TRAVELS IN THE SOUT

FLYING AROUND 8 COUNTRIES OF THE PACIFIC

JASON SMART

Text and Photographs Copyright © 2018 Jason Smart

All Rights Reserved. No part of this book may be reproduced or transmitted in any form or by any means, electronic or mechanical, including photocopying, recording, or any information storage and retrieval system, without prior written permission of the Author.

First English edition published in 2018 by Smart Travel Publishing

The moral right of Jason J Smart to be identified as the author of this work had been asserted in accordance with the Copyright, Designs and Patents Act, 1988

Cover design by Ace Graphics

Smart, Jason J
Travels in the South Pacific

Dedicated to Andrew Billington: a true gentleman; taken far too early

ALSO BY JASON SMART

The Red Quest
Flashpacking through Africa
The Balkan Odyssey
Panama City to Rio de Janeiro
Temples, Tuk-tuks & Fried Fish Lips
Bite Size North America
Rapid Fire Europe
Crowds, Colour, Chaos
Meeting the Middle East
From Here to Anywhere
Africa to Asia
An Accidental Tourist
Hola, Amigo
Take Your Wings and Fly

Port Moresby, PAPUA NEW GUINEA
Honiara, SOLOMON ISLANDS
Port Vila, VANUATU
Nadi, FIJI
Nuku'alofa, TONGA
Auckland, NEW ZEALAND
Apia, SAMOA
Dili, TIMOR LESTE

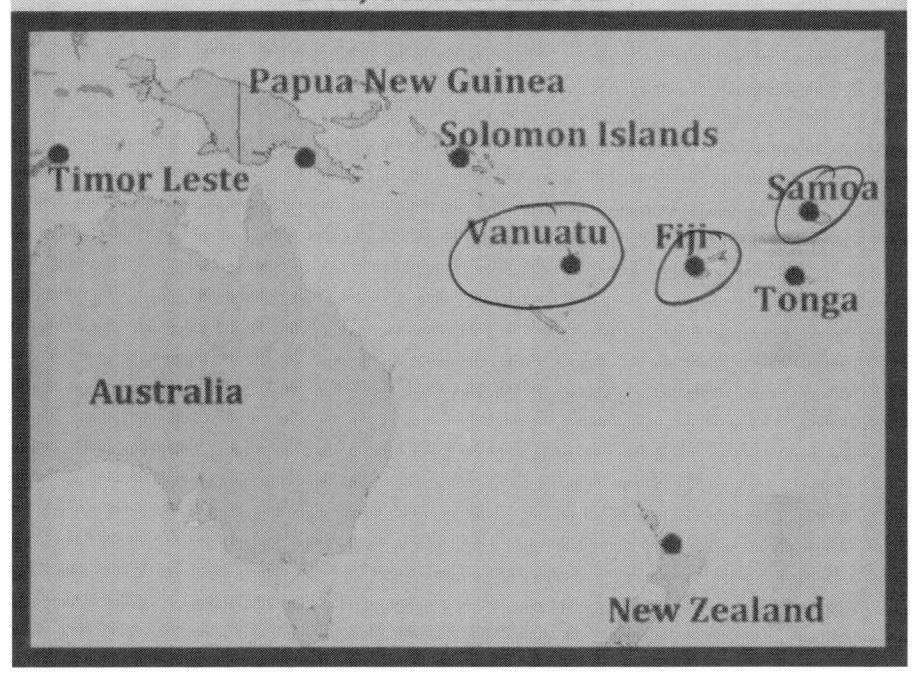

Contents:

Chapter 1.   Port Moresby, Papua New Guinea..................1

Chapter 2.   Honiara, Solomon Islands 38

Chapter 3.   Port Vila, Vanuatu 65

Chapter 4.   Nadi, Fiji 89

Chapter 5.   Nuku'alofa, Tonga 113

Chapter 6.   Auckland, New Zealand 137

Chapter 7.   Apia, Samoa 151

Chapter 8.   Dili, East Timor/Timor-Leste 175

Jason Smart

Travels in the
SOUTH PACIFIC

SMART TRAVEL PUBLISHING
MANCHESTER

Chapter 1. Port Moresby, Papua New Guinea

Interesting fact: When a Spanish explorer visited the islands and noted how the people looked similar to the people of Guinea in West Africa, he called this land New Guinea.

"Jeez, mate, you're flying to Port Moresby?" said the incredulous young man behind one of the wallet-busting sandwich counters at Brisbane International Airport. He had just scanned my Air Niugini boarding card so I could purchase a ham and cheese croissant for twenty dollars.

I nodded, pulling him a strained, thin-lipped, smile as I handed over my cash. Why a ham and cheese croissant should cost twenty dollars was beyond my comprehension.

The man, whose nametag identified him as Troy, opened his till and placed my money on top of the piles already there. After putting my croissant in his microwave, he turned back to me. "My older brother works out there. He hates it. He says he drives to work a different route every day in case bad guys are following him. He's got bullet-proof windows and a panic button in his car. He tells me it's like a war zone in Port Moresby, and the only reason he goes there is because of the money. Danger money, he calls it. But I suppose you know this already, yeah? You wouldn't be going if you didn't know the score, right?"

"Yeah," I answered noncommittally, even though my innards were swirling like soup. Troy had put into words my nervousness at flying to Papua New Guinea's edgy capital city, a place to avoid according to the media.

In a recent poll, Port Moresby ranked at number three in a list of Worst Places in the World to Live. Only Lagos in Nigeria and Damascus in Syria beat it to the top spot.

Numerous travel advisories warn of the extreme violence that could befall a visitor foolish enough to step off a plane in Port Moresby. The chance of being robbed was alarmingly high as was the likelihood of being carjacked. Shootings and stabbings were common in the city; the main perpetrators: young, disenfranchised local men. With unemployment running at over sixty percent, coupled with a non-existent welfare system, youths living in Port Moresby's squatter communities joined street gangs and called themselves raskols. They were becoming a big problem in Port Moresby.

The microwave pinged, and Troy turned to get my breakfast. I didn't fancy my croissant now – that much was sure, so I asked him to wrap it so I could take it to the gate.

Once there, I sat and brooded. There was no getting away from it: Port Moresby had a bad reputation and, in hindsight, I should not be going. But I had no one to blame but myself. When I booked my trip around the Pacific Ocean, Papua New Guinea had been a mysterious land to me. Instead of raskols, the name of the country had conjured images of steamy rainforests, verdant hillsides and remote jungle tribes. What it didn't conjure was violence and mayhem on an epic scale. Only after I had booked my flights around the region, did I look into what Papua New Guinea was actually like, and what I discovered horrified me. When I read about the raskols and the carjackings, I wanted to omit it from my trip, but I couldn't; it was too late. Without Port Moresby, I could not get to Honiara in the Solomon Islands. Without Honiara, I would miss my flight to Port Vila in Vanuatu.

So, unless I wanted to cancel the whole trip, I had no choice but to batten down the hatches and sneak into Papua New Guinea without the raskols noticing.

Despite their playful and impish name, raskols are anything but appealing. Crimes of choice for these gang members include rape, murder and carjacking. The former arising mainly as part of a raskol initiation ceremony whereby a teenage gang member, who wants to move up the chain of command and be seen as a real man, will rape a woman or girl. Afterwards, to evade arrest, he will probably murder the victim lest she identifies him. Not that he would be caught; the police in Papua New Guinea are notorious for their lacklustre response to any crime: there is just too much of it to deal with; especially against women.

Papua New Guinea is perhaps the worst place in the world for a woman to live. Estimates suggest that half of the women in the county have been raped or sexually assaulted. In the highlands of the country, this figure is even higher. On the island of Bougainville, one of Papua New Guinea's outlying provinces, a study from 2013 reported that four in every ten men had raped a woman. A fifth admitted to being part of a gang rape.

Up to seventy percent of married women in Papua New Guinea have been beaten so badly by their husbands that they needed medical care. This would be a shocking statistic in most parts of the world but, to the people of Papua New Guinea, it is a shock to no one, least of all the women involved. The country's law does little to help because if a man can prove he was drunk when he punched or stabbed his wife, it will count as an acceptable defence against a charge of spousal abuse.

When asked why they beat their womenfolk, husbands often claim their wives made decisions without consultation, or else caused a family argument. Whenever this happens, men in Papua New Guinea feel the need to assert authority by using their fists. God forbid the wife who goes shopping, buys some ingredients and then cooks a new, but less tasty, meal for her spouse. Heaven help her if she uses the family cash to buy the children some new clothes. Sons will regularly see their fathers beating mothers or sisters and will grow up thinking it is normal behaviour. Hospitals in Papua New Guinea cannot cope with the constant stream of battered women arriving at their doors. Even the Family Protection Act of 2013, making it illegal for a man to abuse his wife, has not stopped the entrenched abuse going on towards the women of Papua New Guinea.

3

The Air Niugini Boeing 737 left the gate on time, and soon I was on my way to PNG, to give it its punchier title. My fellow passengers did not look like raskols and seemed perfectly respectable. Most I guessed were Papua New Guineans, the women with frizzy hair and colourful dresses; the men wearing suits and smiles. Apart from me, there were only two westerners on board: an older Australian gentleman and a teenage girl travelling alone. Back in Brisbane, I had chatted to the Aussie gent during check-in. He told me he worked as a pilot in the wilds of the Papua New Guinean jungle ferrying miners around. When I asked whether he felt safe in the country, the Australian told me he felt safe most of the time, except in Port Moresby, where he spent as little time as possible.

The bush pilot was now sitting behind me somewhere, but the girl was about four rows ahead. She seemed too young to be flying for work, but she did not look like a tourist either. I wondered whether she was a backpacker who knew no fear or someone escaping justice in Australia. If that was the case, then she was certainly heading in the right direction.

Growing bored despite the danger I faced on a distant horizon, I looked out of the window, staring down at the Great Barrier Reef, its mesmerising colours momentarily bewitching me from moroseness. I'd once read that staring at the ocean could change a person's brain wave frequencies, sending them into a mild sedative state. Whether this was true or not, I felt a little calmer, but not enough to remove the sense of terrible foreboding bubbling in the pit of my stomach. A few months previously I had been snorkelling down there with my wife. It was a world away from where I was heading.

Ninety minutes later, a looming landmass appeared over the horizon, and I gazed down with apprehensive interest. Despite what I knew, Papua New Guinea's southern coastline looked inviting: a tropical ocean lapping between remote green headlands. In some of the bays, tiny stilt villages lay, unconnected by road or even track. Behind the headlands, the hinterland was a rough carpet of jagged, luxuriant hills sliced by dramatic valleys. It was an environment Indiana Jones would thrive unless cannibals had captured him.

Unbelievably, cannibalism was only outlawed in Papua New Guinea fifty years ago. Before that, roasting and feasting on human flesh (curiously known as long pig) was a fairly common event, especially in remote parts of the country. And the way they cooked the human meal often went like this: first, a person would be dispatched and chopped into manageable pieces. While this was going on, men with spades would toil over a deep pit, large enough to house the chunks of human. When the hole was big enough, they would toss in burning stones, followed by the freshly cut flesh. On top of the meat, health-conscious cannibals would add layers of vegetables, perhaps yams, followed by another layer of hot rocks. To keep in the heat and juices, someone would liberally sprinkle a cover of banana leaves on top. And then the barbecue from hell would do its magic for the next few hours.

While the cooking and digging crew took a well-deserved breather, the womenfolk of the cannibal tribe would gather plates, cutlery and napkins. Everyone would be licking their lips, looking forward to the feast, especially the chief who would get the chunkiest and choicest bits of the roast, including the brain if he was feeling particularly peckish. And the whole tribe would be involved in the feast: it was a good way for everyone to have a pleasant catch-up and a natter. If they were lucky, they might get some bones to use as ornaments.

But then, at the end of World War II, Australia took over Papua New Guinea and put a stop to the cannibal feasts of fun, pointing out that they were barbaric and inhumane. And if they caught anyone cooking a person, they would throw them in prison for a long time. So all over the nation, cannibals laid down their special knives and forks and lamented that their traditional Papua New Guinean feast had died a sudden death.

Except it hadn't

Occasionally, stories surface that the practice continues. In 2002, an Australian newspaper published a story about a group of villagers. The group had grown annoyed at another group of people who kept turning up in their village demanding money and sexual favours in return for supernatural protection. It was the last bit which made them particularly angry and, believing the unwelcome visitors to be sorcerers, they banded together and killed them. Then they dug a big pit. After a few hours, the long pig meal was ready and, as a starter, platefuls of raw brain were served closely followed by a batch of penis soup. It was only when the police arrived to find out what had happened to the visitors that the truth came out. "We ate them," the village chief possibly said, smacking his lips together.

"Ate them?"

"Yep. With some yams. They were delicious."

"But you can't eat people. It's against the law."

And that was the problem. The village was so remote that no one had bothered to tell the people living there.

4

From the air, Port Moresby looked ragtag and isolated, completely cut off from the rest of the country. Indeed, the only methods of getting into the capital were to trek through the jungle, arrive by boat or, like me, come by plane. The landing was smooth, unlike my innards which were in turmoil. Raskols, cannibals, sorcerers: all were present in the nation I was about to step into, and there was a high chance I would meet at least one of them.

Immigration was straightforward and quick, and the customs officer soon issued me with a full-page yellow visa in my passport. He had not asked why I was in the country and did not seem interested in me at all. Through the other side, with my luggage in tow, I noticed the teenage girl standing at a money-changing booth with an older western man who had not been on the flight: her father, I assumed.

The man was about fifty, lean and wearing a biker jacket that proclaimed he was part of the Port Moresby Motor Cycle Club. When I stood behind them so I could change some dollars into kina, the man in the jacket looked me over and nodded. I smiled back, waiting for the girl to finish so I could begin.

"In PNG for work?" the man asked in a thick Aussie accent.

"Yeah," I offered, not wanting to admit I was here on holiday.

"In Moresby?"

"Yeah. Just for a couple of days. What about you?" I wanted to change the subject from my so-called employment.

"Oh, I live over here, mate. Been in PNG for six years now: work in construction. Abigail is over here for a week to see her old man. By the way, where's your company putting you up?"

"The Grand Papua Hotel."

"Nice. You stayed there before?

"No, this is my first time in Port Moresby."

The man nodded, and Abigail turned to face us. She looked a little bit bored, giving that look only teenagers can give when someone is holding up their essential plans. Her father ignored her. "You sound like a Brit, mate?"

"That's right."

"Not too many Brits over here. The Grand Papua's a good hotel, downtown. Just be careful after dark. Listen to your driver; he'll tell you what's what."

The man must have seen the worry etched across my face.

"Look, the media paints Moresby as the most violent place this side of Iraq, but it's not that bad. Just keep your wits, your head down and vary your routes to work – straightforward stuff your company's probably already told you. Most of the violent crime is centred in the squatter camps when some neighbour pisses off another neighbour and they get the machetes out. That type of thing happens all the time. That and carjackings. They're becoming a bit of problem."

I asked whether he had been carjacked.

The man shook his head. "I'm too careful. I never go out after dark."

I looked at his daughter. Abigail seemed unfazed by the conversation and indeed had deemed it so dull that she was on her phone.

With nothing more to be said on the matter, the man wished me farewell and walked off with his daughter. As for me, I was seriously reconsidering my plans about staying in the Grand Papua and pondering whether I should stay at the airport for a couple of days instead. It would be uncomfortable and annoying, but at least I'd be safe. But if Abigail was brave enough to hit of the streets of Port Moresby, then so was I. After I changed some cash, I headed to arrivals with acute trepidation.

5

If there had not been a man standing there with my name written on a board, I honestly don't know what I would have done. I wouldn't have taken a chance with a regular taxi driver. Not with my nerves jangling like trip wires. But there was a man with my name and he was called Sam.

I shook hands with Sam and headed off to his minibus. He was a thick-set, bald Papuan man in his late fifties. His features reminded me of the indigenous peoples of Australia, as did his accent, which had a definite Aussie twang. Keeping a wary eye out for potential troublemakers, I climbed into the back of Sam's minibus, hiding my luggage out of sight but close to hand in case I had to use it as a walloping device. When Sam climbed into the front, I surveyed the outside of Jackson International Airport, which looked like any other airport in the world. People were emerging from the main building shielding their eyes from the sharp midday sun. A woman with a floppy hat was lighting a cigarette while a man carrying a briefcase walked purposefully toward a taxi. No one shot at them from the shadows or tried to eat their brains. It was all perfectly normal.

Aside from the initial hello when I'd first encountered him, Sam had said very little. As we set off, he switched on the radio and I wondered whether the windows were of bullet-proof glass and so asked.

"Bulletproof? No, mate, Just regular glass," came the jovial answer.

I looked outside at the street we were traversing. It was a commercial district with a couple of hardware shops and a sizeable JMart store. Some people were walking along the side of the road carrying boxes of shopping, their packages either balanced on their heads or grasped in front of them. The customers of JMart did not own cars it seemed. One car did overtake us, though. Its occupant was a single male who looked as law-abiding as everyone else. Even so, I was still on edge. Especially now that I knew the minibus didn't have protective glass.

"What about a panic button?" I asked.

Sam laughed. "No mate, nothing like that."

"So is it safe driving here?" I could not remember a time where I had felt such a keen edge of disquiet. It was a feeling I was not enjoying.

"Alright man, let's talk. I'm never sure whether a client wants to talk or not, so I think it's best to keep quiet until I know for sure. But you seem like a talker." He switched off the radio. I smiled thinly, warming to the driver's casual manner but not enough to relax.

"You were asking if it's safe driving in the city. The answer is yes and no. These main roads are fine, even at night. But unlit roads or roads that pass through the squatter camps are not."

I took in this information. It made sense, sort of. I said, "But I've heard that carjackings happen all over the place, especially at traffic intersections. Has that happened to you?"

"Never been carjacked once in thirty years of driving. But they do happen. Usually, it's three or four guys working as a team. One will wait in the middle of the road so a passing car slows down, and then the others will jump out and rob it. I've read they sometimes throw eggs at a windscreen so the car has to stop, but that's a new one – they're always thinking up new ways. Another new one is leaving a doll in a cot by the side of the road. A concerned citizen thinks it's an abandoned baby and they'll stop. That's when the gang rushes in. But they don't usually kill people; they rough them up, steal their stuff and go on their way. Back in the 90s, it was foreigners they went for, but nowadays it's mainly our middle class they're after."

We stopped at a traffic light intersection. I scanned the area in all directions. No one was running towards us with a gun. When the lights turned green, all was well again and we moved into the heart of Baghdad, I mean Port Moresby.

6

We pulled up outside the Grand Papua Hotel's tall metal gates, each section topped with barbed wire. The presence of security cameras and armed guards cheered me. Sam, I noted, did not stop near the gate but kept a fair bit of room in front of us. I assumed this was because the gates swung outward and he did not want the front of his minibus dented. But I was wrong.

"Every driver knows not to pull in too close to a wall or a gate; we need an exit plan. A lot of carjackers know that if they want to rob someone, the best place is just outside a person's compound. If a car pulls right up at the gate, it's stuck and can't go anywhere. That's when the bad guys come up behind and get them. But, because I've parked a few feet away, if I see anyone coming, I can get away."

"You should train people to drive here."

Sam found this funny and laughed. "Maybe I should."

Sam didn't seem to be looking around for raskols, and so I did it for him, also watching the hotel's security guards as they slid the gate open. Like me, they were scouring our surroundings for potential assailants. To my left was a group of high rise buildings, mainly banks and commercial offices. To my right was a line of faded storefronts. If any muggers lurked, then that would be their hiding place. Indeed, a few men were sitting under the shade near the shops, but none seemed interested in us. A couple of mangy brown dogs plodded along the street, sniffing the dust and palm tree trunks. One picked up a stray piece of litter and then discarded it a metre further along. A group of children ran past carrying sticks and raucous laughter. A minivan stopped to pick up some passengers. Among them was an old lady wearing a large hat. She did not seem like a gangland goon. We drove forward into the hotel car park and the security guards closed the gates behind us, locking them tight. It was like I was in a heist movie.

Now that I had reached the safety of the protected car park, I felt an unexpected wave of relief wash over me. I felt almost giddy with delight but then suddenly felt weary. The adrenalin that had been coursing through my body had now gone and I needed to lie down and take stock. With the next day to fill, the most significant decision I needed to make was whether I was going to wait it out in the hotel all day or go out and see the city. Sam seemed to read my mind. "So what are your plans for tomorrow?"

I told him I was thinking of taking a tour of the city. "Or is that a stupid idea?"

"No way, mate. It's a great idea. I'd take you out myself, but I've got a whole load of airport runs to make. Ask at the desk; they'll help you out with organising a tour." Sam stopped and looked at his watch. "Tell you what, though, I can take you out on a little walk this afternoon, just around here. I can point out a couple of things in town and show you how friendly we all are. No charge, either. I'm not doing my next airport run for another few hours so I have plenty of time."

I pondered Sam's proposal. He was a good guy, that much was evident, but did I trust him enough to take me into the mean streets of Port Moresby. Maybe he had accomplices who would rob and maim me away from the protection of the hotel security cameras. Perhaps there was a large pot around the corner filled with carrots and potatoes which just needed some meat. But if Sam's motive was less than honourable, then he was going the wrong way about it. The best time to rob me had passed. My belongings were now inside the hotel grounds, protected by gun-wielding security guards. Surely if he intended to take them, he would have organised my beating on the way from the airport. No, Sam was not going to assemble a gang of raskols to do me over: he was genuine. So I decided to take him up on his offer, just as soon as I'd had some lunch. Besides, what was the alternative? Hide away in my hotel room quivering in fright for the rest of the day? Actually, that sounded quite appealing.

Just before I headed into the hotel, Sam stopped me. "See down there?" He was pointing at a small car park opposite a few shops. A couple of cars were there, perhaps customers for Yummy Chicken or the Kai Bar, which did not serve booze, but fast food. Someone inside the Kai Bar was selling greasy chicken and chips through a protective wire mesh hatch. "A couple of months back, an Aussie was shot in the arse in that car park."

I looked at Sam.

"He'd just come out of the bank around the corner and was about to get in his car when another car pulled up and some bloke shot him in the arse." Sam tried to stifle a snigger. "I don't think he was aiming for his arse, but that's where he got him. The Aussie didn't go down, though; he managed to hobble across the street to the Chamber of Commerce. He ended up in hospital. He was okay, but he couldn't sit down for a week or two."

"What about the robber?"

"Drove off."

"And did the police catch him?"

"I don't think so. I doubt they even bothered trying; the Aussie bloke wasn't killed or anything."

I considered the story. "What time of day did this happen?"

"Broad daylight. About lunchtime."

I scoffed. "And you're telling me it's safe to walk around here this afternoon. You're not exactly instilling me with confidence, Sam."

"That bloke had just been to the bank. The bad guy watched him come out and saw his chance. But you'll be with me, and you won't be bringing anything valuable with you. Leave your wallet and watch in your room. Besides, everyone around here knows Sam."

7

My room was nice. From the balcony, I enjoyed a panoramic view of the Pacific Ocean and a smattering of skyscrapers that made up the capital's central business district. The beach in the near distance looked like it was under some development but still looked inviting despite the littering of diggers. If Port Moresby could sort out its crime and build some resort hotels, it could be a top-end destination. Maybe.

After lunch, I met Sam in reception. Together, we walked out the back of the hotel where the same security guards were still watching the street. Before we entered the Badlands, I peered through the metal bars. A shirtless man was sitting under a fast food shack, head down, perhaps asleep. Further along, a couple of men in baseball caps were standing and doing nothing in particular. One flicked a cigarette end into the road. Just then, a car trundled past and stopped at the intersection near them. None of the loiterers ran at it with a gun or machete. They stayed put, continuing with their pastime of doing very little.

The thin road outside the hotel was called Douglas Street and I decided to go for it, following Sam. With the security gates firmly closed behind us, we were on our own, walking past the Kai Bar and the car park where a raskol had shot an Australian man in the left buttock. The idling men across the street glanced our way but did nothing else. At the intersection, a blue and white minibus pulled up and obediently waited for the green light even though it was the only vehicle in attendance. When the lights changed, it rolled forward a few metres and disgorged a few passengers, mainly women with shopping bags. The group of frizzy-haired old folk walked towards a dainty white Catholic church called St Mary's. It was one of the city's oldest places of worship but looked brand new. The best thing about it was its tall, pointed entranceway covered in a paint job so wacky that it would have looked good on an African tribal mask. In fact, the whole street, from the fume-belching minibus to the loitering people and litter, reminded me of cities I'd visited in West Africa.

Seeing old ladies entering the church lifted my spirits. How dangerous could a place be if a trio of elderly women could ride in a minibus and then walk along a street without anything untoward happening? I turned to Sam. "Port Moresby seems okay so far."

Sam smiled. "I told you it would be. But this is daylight. Everything's fine right now."

"So what would it be like at night?"

We were walking past the church, heading downhill towards the coast. There were a few more people, mostly kids, making their way to the beach. "That's when bad blokes hang around. It's not too bad here because they know that anyone with a brain has gone home to their compound or is tucked up inside their hotel. But I would not recommend leaving the hotel after sundown."

We turned right, following dual carriageway bordered by a hill on one side and the beach on the other. The hill housed relics from World War II: artillery emplacements, tunnels and other harbour defences that the Australian military built to repel a potential

Japanese invasion. Today, the emplacements are empty but Sam told me there was talk of redeveloping the whole hillside area.

"I've seen plans for what the Government wants to do to Paga Hill," he told me. "There'll be a hotel, a museum, some restaurants and a new cruise ship jetty down here somewhere. I think the Aussies are paying for some of it. But some people are not happy, especially all the folk on top of the hill being forced out of their houses."

"Who is at all for, though? I mean, are you expecting lots of tourists to start coming to Port Moresby?"

"Don't ask me. I doubt it, though."

Because it was Sunday, the beach was busy. Families were either sloshing about in small wooden boats, swimming in the shallows or paddling around tentatively at the edge of the water. Fathers were playing with children while mothers sat on the beach and chatted. If I had not known about Papua New Guinea's underbelly of family violence, I would never have guessed by what I would see at the beach. Sounds of joy abounded from everywhere and, because nobody was giving me a second glance, I found I was enjoying myself.

Around the other side of the beach was the harbour area, an ugly place of fences, ships and warehouses. But upon another hill were some of the nicest homes of Port Moresby: large dwellings surrounded by tall walls, solid fences, security cameras and panic alarms. According to Sam, they were where politicians, government ministers and heads of companies lived: all of them prisoners by night. After a quick zip across the road, I found our walk had looped us around a small headland and we were now heading back towards the Grand Papua.

"Do you think crime's getting worse than it was?" I asked.

Sam considered this for a moment. Just then a small group of boys, aged about ten, approached us. They glanced at Sam and smiled. They stopped said something but I couldn't understand. Later I learned the language was *Tok Pisin*, a local form pidgin based on German, English and Melanesian. Sam conferred with them, which made them all laugh. A few glanced in my direction. They were soon on their raucous way.

"No, I don't think crime's getting worse. It's bad, but ten years ago it was worse. Foreigners didn't feel safe here, but now it's not so bad."

"But could this be because foreigners are more aware of crime and have taken steps to avoid it?"

"Maybe. Foreign companies tell their fellas about safety stuff now; so yeah, that probably helps. Most fellas who come here know they shouldn't stop their car if they get a puncture. They know to not drive at night or, if they have to, they go in a convoy or with an armed guard. But one thing you've got to remember – and I keep saying this – is most people in my country don't want to hurt you. It's just a few bad apples who are spoiling it for everyone."

We walked up the gradient towards the hotel in silence for a few moments. Then I asked Sam what he had said to the kids to make them laugh.

"Oh, those are good boys. I know their mothers. I was telling them to get home and help with the chores or I'd kick their arses."

We entered the hotel where I retired to my room for the remainder of the evening. Maybe Port Moresby wasn't as dangerous as I thought.

8

The next morning I opened the curtains and looked outside. The sun was bathing Port Moresby in tropical light and everything in the central core seemed to be operating as usual. So my choices were to stay in my room all day, where I would be safe, or to venture out into the danger to see a few things like a fish market, the botanical gardens and maybe a stilt village. I sighed deeply, weighing up the options. Ordinarily, the choice would have been easy, but I was in no ordinary city. I decided to speak to the hotel desk staff to ask for advice.

The woman behind the reception desk told me that a city tour was possible, but suggested I use a company called Black Swan. "They are the only drivers we recommend for our guests. You can find out more over there."

She was pointing to a couple of iPads mounted on stands near the entrance. They both showed the Black Swan homepage. I could only presume that the company had paid to fit them there. Their website told me I needed to download their app; I did so and returned to my room to do some research.

Black Swan possessed a slick and unusual corporate message: *security solutions specifically tailored to meet the unique threats of the PNG environment.* I didn't care for the words 'unique threats', but was pleased when they pointed out that their company was the only one in the country that was 'fully security-aware'. To back up this claim, all their vehicles came with fully trained drivers, GPS tracking devices and panic buttons. From their city headquarters, Black Swan could track all their cars and, if need be, have armed assistance in place within minutes.

Wow, I thought, reading through their website. Did I need all this to do a bit of sightseeing? Was Port Moresby that bad? Perhaps it was. Maybe my little walk with Sam the previous day had lulled me into thinking the city was okay. But that trip had been around the hotel area: the relatively safe central core of business. Maybe the streets further out were dangerous. Maybe raskols were lurking there right now. I looked at how much it would cost to book a Black Swan car for a few hours. They offered a number of options.

The cheapest choice was to hire a car and driver. This would suffice for a quick, last-minute trip, the website suggested. However, for a measure of extra safety or a longer trip, it might be prudent to have an unmarked escort car following in case of a carjacking attempt. This would be more expensive but if I valued my life, then it might be money well spent. But there was still another choice: the granddaddy of Black Swan's options. For a king's ransom, an armed security guard could come along on the trip so I could pretend I was in Mogadishu.

I wrote a request for the cheapest option and sent off the online form. Ten minutes later, a quote arrived for a four-hour trip and I almost fell off my chair. For that price, I could fly back to Brisbane. When I went down to reception and told the woman the price, she looked a little shocked. "Yes, they're expensive but, as I said before, they're the only company we can genuinely recommend. They have all the correct insurance and will keep you safe."

I nodded. "Do you think I need them? Is the city that dangerous?"

The woman pulled a stern face. "Unfortunately yes, the city can be dangerous, and Black Swan is the only company we recommend." She seemed stuck on repeat.

"So I can't just order a regular taxi?"

"I would not advise that, sir."

"But you must use regular taxis sometimes?" I pressed.

The woman admitted that the hotel did sometimes do that.

"So can I order one of these taxis?"

"You can, but we strongly advise you, as one of our hotel guests, to use the services of Black Swan. Are you sure you want to risk things by travelling in a regular taxi?"

It was a good question and one I had to consider carefully; after all, I had no experience of what it would be like on the trip. Perhaps Black Swan ought to be my only option because if anything *did* happen to me in a regular taxi, then I would lambast myself evermore for being a cheapskate. I thanked the woman and walked away; resigning myself to the expensive hit I would take on my wallet. As I did so, the receptionist called me over again.

"Look, I understand your predicament and, while we always recommend Black Swan, I can organise a regular driver that the hotel staff sometimes use. His car is unmarked, so you'll be safe. His price is much lower than Black Swan – maybe around 100 kina for four hours. How does that sound?"

One hundred kina was about twenty-five pounds, a fraction of Black Swan's quote. But now that the offer was on the table, I suddenly felt apprehensive. Should I go for cheap and cheerful or expensive and safe? I decided to bite the bullet and told the hotel receptionist that the taxi would be great. I just hoped I would not have to bite a bullet for real.

9

Jack, the taxi driver, was in his mid-fifties, grey-haired and, like Sam, in possession of the same features as most men I'd seen in Port Moresby: dark skin, broad nose and stocky body. He also looked like a seasoned betel nut chewer: reddish lips and stained teeth from its juices.

Betel nuts come from the areca tree, a plant common around certain Pacific islands. The nut is actually a berry but contains something called arecoline, a stimulant that offers a sense of euphoria to anyone who chews it. People start young with their betel nut appreciation in Papua New Guinea, and it's not unusual to see children munching them, with red saliva leaking out of their mouths. Red blotches cover pavements across the city where people have spat its juice onto the ground. More than half the population of the country is a regular chewer of betel nuts.

Jack wasn't chewing at this moment as he led me to his car. Like the receptionist had said, there were no markings on it to suggest it was a taxi, and I was further pleased to note it had darkened windows. Jack seemed an affable fellow and told me that he lived close to one of the squatter camps in Port Moresby. "I know a few raskols," he told me. "The thing is, if you hide away from them, they'll come for you. But if they know you – and know your family – they'll leave you alone."

We drove to the Koki Fish Market, a hotbed of tuna, silverfish and mud crabs. On route, I looked at other road users and deduced they were law-abiding, as were the people walking around. No one was looking at our car with intent: they were not bothered; too busy with their own lives. When we parked outside the fish market, Jack told me to look around while he waited by the car to have a cigarette.

"Is it safe to go in by myself?" I asked.

"Totally safe, mate. I'll be waiting right here."

I took a deep breath and stepped out of the car into the heat of the morning. The Koki Fish Market was at the end of a small jetty. Across from it, on the other side of a narrow bay, lay a collection of stilt houses, many with washing dangling from string lines. A couple of kids were playing underneath the homes, kicking water at one another. I walked to the market's large open-air entrance where a sign warned that smoking cigarettes and chewing betel nuts were not allowed. Marbling the ground near the sign were tell-tale blotches of red. It looked like someone had been murdered. Maybe they had. I stepped over the red mess and entered.

I was the only white guy in attendance and was soon the centre of attention from the vendors. Smiles, waves and shout of hello all came my way. "Where you from?" asked a man in charge of the mud crab stall. About two hundred of them were laid out on a table covered in mud.

"England."

"England? Long way, mate."

I smiled and nodded. "How much are the crabs?"

"Small ones: five kina, big ones: six. You want one?"

Five kina was about £1.20. I watched the man pick a specimen up. He thrust it toward me. I had assumed the crabs were dead, but they weren't. This was alive, if not entirely kicking. I felt immediately sorry for it.

"No thanks, I'm just enjoying looking around."

"You sure? They're delicious."

I shook my head and smiled.

"Well, take your time. And thanks for coming to Port Moresby." He put the crab back on the pile and busied himself checking that the rest of his wares were securely tied. Another man, this one in charge of a stall that peddled elongated silver fish with fearsome arrays of serrated teeth asked me what I was doing in the city.

"Just visiting."

"As a tourist?"

I nodded.

"And you came here?" He shook his head at the notion and nudged his sleepy neighbour, a woman in charge of the parrot fish stall. "This fella here's from England!"

The woman looked me up and down but said nothing.

The silver fish seller said, "I don't think we've had a tourist from England here in ten years. Mind you, I don't think we've had any tourists here for years, full stop. So well done, mate."

Back outside, smiling at the friendly exchanges I'd received, I walked up to a giant fish sculpture at the far end of the car park. Its head, tail and dorsal fin were all solid chunks of metal, but the body was made up of curved rib-like pieces of steel. It was sizeable enough that a couple of young men were able to sit inside. I didn't notice them at first, but as I angled for a photograph, their stares came to my attention. "Hi," I said.

Both smiled back and returned the greeting.

"Can I take a photo?" I asked.

They looked at each other and shrugged. The men posed inside the stomach of the empty metal fish, smiling into the camera. As I pressed the button, one of them formed his hand into the shape of a gun. He pointed it at his pal.

10

"Black Swan is muscling in on us regular blokes," said Jack as we drove away from the city centre. The traffic was light with more pedestrians than cars. Most people were ambling under brightly-coloured sun parasols or else waiting for minibuses to turn up. A few people were outside a shop called KNC Fast Food: It's the Best Taste in PNG, it proudly declared.

"Black Swan makes out – to people like you – that you *need* their service and if you don't book with them, you'll be in danger. It's a crock of shit, mate. Sure, they've got the big cars and the panic buttons, but so what? I know the roads better than them, and I know where the bad blokes hang out. If you'd hired a Black Swan car, I'm telling you, you'd be wasting your money."

Jack slowed down and pointed at a series of large, low-level buildings that collectively made up something called the Fortune Club. One part of the complex was an eatery called the Imperial Restaurant. Behind it, unseen from the road, was a bar and a gambling house. "There was a bad shooting there a couple of months back," Jack told me. "The manager of the restaurant, a Malaysian bloke, was leaving with the night's takings. As he drove off, some raskol shot him. The bloke managed to drive away a bit, but then crashed. The raskol ran and shot him some more; killed him so he could take the cash."

I shook my head. "Did they catch the robber?"

"No, but they reckon he's dead, anyway. A couple of weeks after robbing this place, he was robbing somewhere else and ended up being shot by security guards."

I sighed. "Stories like this will stop tourists coming to Papua New Guinea. Why don't the police do something?"

"There are not enough of them on the streets." By now, we had turned off the main road and were driving through a quieter part of town full of palm trees and fences. If I were paranoid, I thought it might be an excellent place to stage of robbery.

"How many police officers are there in Port Moresby?"

"I don't know, but we have one the lowest ratios of cops in the world."

He was correct about this because I checked. According to official figures released in 2012, Papua New Guinea had just 65 serving police officers per 100,000 people, putting it a snip ahead of Somalia, which came out with 55 officers. To put this figure into perspective, nations such as Norway, Australia, Japan and Iceland, where major crimes such as murder, carjacking and rape are seen as abnormalities rather than the norm, employ three times the number of police officers per 100,000 as Papua New Guinea. The country's police force is inadequate for the tasks at hand and the criminals know that. Even reinstating the death penalty in 2015 offered little in the way of a deterrent to Port Moresby's raskol gangs.

Another problem was the police itself. By all accounts, police units were poorly trained and ill-disciplined. Two months before my arrival in Port Moresby, a group of disgruntled officers had gathered outside some city barracks and started shooting. The building was full of other police officers from another department. Thankfully no one was killed and the officers in question were quickly taken into custody. An investigation discovered that a minor argument between both units plus a heavy bout of drinking had escalated into bullets flying. Simply put, a few officers had drunk themselves silly and, instead of sleeping off the effects, had picked up their guns to take some pot-shots at fellow police officers.

Another story was worse. It happened the week I left. After work one day, two police constables decided to have a wild night. Instead of hitting the bars and nightspots of the city, they masqueraded as raskols. But this wasn't an undercover mission; no, it was a mini crime spree of their own making. After removing the number plates from one of their own cars, they drove off in search of opportunity.

Their first victim was a truck driver. They hid their car and then brought his lorry to a standstill, waving their guns around. Believing them to be raskols, the driver relinquished his mobile phone and cargo of betel nuts. After throwing the driver onto the side of the road, the rogue cops commandeered his truck and drove away, chewing away on betel nuts. Sometime later, the pair decided to shoot at a man at random. He happened to be in the wrong place at the wrong time. After taking a pot-shot from the truck window, the cops were pleased to see him go down, severely injured. After this, the fake raskols drove to a nightclub so they could do some partying. And this is what they did for the rest of the night until fellow officers barged in and arrested them on suspicion of armed robbery and attempted murder.

And these were two members of the nation's law enforcement team, meant to be protecting the good people of Papua New Guinea

11

The palm trees thinned and a large building came into view: the National Parliament House of Papua New Guinea. It was set back inside a tall fence and surrounded by well-tended foliage. A metallic golden bird of paradise guarded the curved gates that formed its closed entrance, the bird's feathers spilling out across the railings. There was another bird of paradise on the nation's flag, which was hanging limply on a tall post near the building. Always a top-20 winner in flag design polls, a fifteen-year-old girl had designed the emblem before entering it in a 1971 competition. Her winning design was a rectangle split diagonally into two black and red triangles. In the black section, the five stars of the Southern Cross contrasted with the golden bird of paradise in the red. I climbed out of the car so I could take a photo of the flag.

The distant parliament house was also worthy of a photograph. It looked curiously familiar: the distinctive gradient of the roof; the traditional art-style markings that formed the entrance and the vertical windows that resembled shark gills – they were something I'd seen before. And then it came to me. I fished out a banknote from my wallet and compared the image to reality. The parliament building was on the rear side of every kina banknote. I looked to see if any politicians were walking about, but I could see no one. But that was because it was Sunday.

In 1971, the parliament of Papua New Guinea had been busy at work coming up with an almost unbelievable piece of legislation. It was called the Sorcery Act: an outlandish ruling that did not banish the belief in magic and fairy dust, but endorsed it.

For centuries, the people of Papua New Guinea have believed in 'white' and 'black' magic. 'White' magic was the act of healing someone through prayers or by using charms whereas 'black' magic was the dark art of casting a spell on someone to cause the victim discomfort, injury or even death. The Sorcery Act made it a crime to commit these 'black' magic acts. Anyone who did so would be arrested for being a witch or a sorcerer. So, while belief in witchcraft had ended in Europe and the Americas by the early Nineteenth century, in Papua New Guinea, due to the Sorcery Act, witches, wizards and warlocks continued to be real.

And what was the result of the act? Overnight, prisons became full of sorcerers, especially women. But another terrible consequence of the Sorcery Act was that, because the government had officially stated that witches existed, people felt they could kill them without recourse. Hundreds of women have been murdered every year in Papua New Guinea; many more tortured, due to the Sorcery Act. And these witch killings continue to this day.

In 2008 a story emerged about one gruesome witch killing. A man from the highlands of Papua New Guinea had contracted a terrible disease that left him bedbound and delirious. When a doctor saw him, he diagnosed malaria and told the man's family to take him to a hospital without delay. But it was too late; the diseased man succumbed shortly after. And that should have been that: a tragedy caused by the bite of a mosquito. But, as events transpired, that was not that. The family didn't believe that malaria had killed him and instead thought a local sorceress had stricken him down with a spell. Even with a death certificate saying the cause of death was malaria, members of the man's family captured and tortured the woman until she admitted she was a witch. With the confession came her murder. They burned her to death.

In 2013 another witch killing occurred, a murder so shocking that the world's media got hold of it. When a six-year-old boy died, his mother accused another woman in the village of causing his death by sorcery. The evidence was there for all to see: the woman lived alone, she often acted strangely and she had been caught staring at the boy before his untimely death. This was all the proof the villagers needed and they went in search of the sorceress. After finding the young woman quivering in her home, the mob stripped then tortured her with a hot iron until she confessed she was a witch. Then they dragged the petrified woman to a public rubbish dump and covered her in petrol. Someone lit a match and set her alight. An innocent twenty-year-old woman died an agonising death while the lynch mob blocked anyone, including the police, from helping her. No one has ever been arrested for this crime.

Following this death and another one shortly afterwards where a woman accused of witchcraft was beheaded, the government of Papua New Guinea was forced into action. Looking long and hard at the 1971 Sorcery Act, they finally repealed it; thereby ending the ludicrous situation whereby a murderer could cite killing a sorcerer as a legitimate defence. However, the inherent belief in witches still prevails, especially in parts of the country where traditional village life is mostly untouched by an act of parliament in the city. Indeed, in 2017, a shocking new case of witchcraft emerged when a six-year-old girl was saved from certain death by the actions of a quick-thinking charity worker. A mob of men had gone after the little girl when a local man had suddenly taken ill for no fathomable reason. They believed she had cast a spell in him. After subduing the girl's father, the group took the child and used hot knives to remove the skin from her back in an attempt to weaken her powers. When the charity worker witnessed the horrific attack, he told the attackers that the ill man was walking around in good health. Instead of feeling guilty, the men took this as a sign they had lessoned the young witch's spell but agreed to stop torturing her. Somehow, the charity worker managed to negotiate the release of the girl and escaped the village with her in his care. She made a full recovery and now lives with her father in an undisclosed location.

I gazed around the peaceful area in which the National Parliament House was located. The sky above it was blue, the breeze soothing and the only sound was of distant traffic. From here, it was hard to imagine terrible deeds going on in a country that still believed in witches.

12

A policeman stopped the car in front of us. Even though the car was a hundred metres away, I could see it was covered in rust and sending out a thick contrail of dark grey smoke from whatever passed as its exhaust system. As Jack and I slowed down behind it, I assumed the cop had flagged the driver down due to the state of his vehicle.

The officer was carrying a large firearm in his hand at waist height. He was in uniform but slovenly dressed: he had not tucked in his shirt; his trousers were unkempt. After a glance at the rusty exterior, the policeman leaned into the driver's window and said something. I glanced at Jack.

"Just a police check, that's all. He'll be checking the bloke isn't carrying a weapon or isn't doing anything bad. He'll probably give us the once-over, too. If he does, don't say anything; let me do the talking."

After a few moments, the police officer stepped back and waved the driver on. It was our turn. Jack rolled down his window and as soon as the policeman saw us, he gestured for us to go. He plodded back to his parked car, totally uninterested in us or the other cars that had formed into a queue.

"You know why that was?" Jack asked.

I shook my head.

"Cos you're a white bloke and he didn't want the hassle. He knows if he did something wrong or said the wrong thing, you might report him. It's not worth his while."

We drove on, negotiating a roundabout and then carried on to the botanical gardens, which turned out to be an oasis of tranquillity within Port Moresby. Instead of concrete, tarmac and litter, there were giant palm trees, nature trails and animals. With Jack waiting for me in the car park, I wandered through, enjoying the sense of almost being in the jungle. When I spied a bird of paradise up in a tree, I almost burst into song.

I was surprised to learn that, like Australia, Papua New Guinea has an abundance of saltwater crocodiles. They lurk furtively along its coastlines. Further inland, it has wallabies and kangaroos, the latter of the tree variety. In the botanical gardens, I was staring at a family of reddish-brown tree kangaroos. They sat huddled inside a spacious tree-clad enclosure, their appearance a pleasing mix of a koala and a regular kangaroo. In another deep enclosed space, I took sight of a cassowary. These rare flightless birds, similar in appearance to ostriches and emus (though smaller than both), reside within the thick rainforests of Papua New Guinea.

The beauty of the cassowary struck me first: its head was a rich mixture of red and blue, with a pair of ruby eyes that seem to swivel in every direction at once. Its neck shimmered in metallic blue, and even the dangling crimson wattle could not take away its attractiveness. I stared at its curious *casque*, a bony ridge sitting on its head like an avian Mohican. Scientists are at a loss to explain the casque. Some say it helps the birds to barge through jungle undergrowth. Others say it acts as a deflecting device should an errant mango drop from above. Perhaps it is a weapon, some scientists suggest, used for fighting off rival males, or maybe it is used a means of cooling the bird down due to its hollow interior. Basically, no one has a clue. But one thing scientists do agree upon are the cassowary's feet and how dangerous they are.

Each large foot has three toes. These are big, meaty toes with sharp claws at the end. The middle toe is the most formidable, with a dagger-like claw five inches long. In 1926, the first and only documented killing by a cassowary happened in Queensland, Australia. Two teenage brothers came across one and decided to hit it with sticks. Instead of retreating, the cassowary cast its malevolent red eyes at the boys and charged, delivering a forward kick to one brother which sent him flying. While this boy rubbed himself down, the other brother, sixteen-year-old Phillip McClean, tried to run away but ended up tripping. While he was down, the cassowary kicked him in the neck, severing his jugular vein. The boy bled to death while the bird escaped from whence it came.

Cassowaries have also attacked dogs, cats and horses. Dogs have been disembowelled by the mad birds. They have also attacked cars and smashed house windows with their dreadful claws, perhaps thinking that their reflection was another cassowary. They can swim, run up to 30mph and can jump five feet in the air. They are the ninja assassins of the rainforest, attacking foragers and passers-by whenever the fancy takes them, which, mercifully, is not very often. In a recent study of all cassowary attacks, researchers could only find evidence of 221 attacks on humans, with just the one mentioned above being fatal. And the biggest single cause of these attacks was the bird wanting food or trying to protect its eggs.

I looked down at the cassowary in Port Moresby's botanic garden enclosure, estimating the height of its home to be about seven feet below me, well away from its murderous claw. Even so, when its red eye singled me out for attention, I shivered and moved on. It was time to leave.

13

Downtown Port Moresby looked down at heel. I think it was the garbage that did the trick. When a city couldn't be bothered cleaning up after itself, and its citizens didn't have any pride in where they lived, this is what happened.

The crossroads Jack and I were presently waiting at typified this look. Ramshackle stalls set under bright parasols littered the intersection. They were selling mainly bottles of water and sun-drenched T-shirts. Because of the stalls, empty plastic bottles lay discarded in the dust, detritus from people waiting for taxis or minibuses. Groups of people hanging around added to the scene of disarray: men were lounging under trees or leaning against traffic barriers. With no job to go to, what else was there for them to do? Plastic bags were everywhere, billowing along the dusty verge, propelled by every passing vehicle. More plastic bags gathered in tree branches or fences like ugly white, misshapen birds. Port Moresby was a litter bin.

"You wanna see a squatter settlement?" asked Jack.

I processed his request and laughed. "You're joking, right?"

The lights changed and we moved forward. "There's one not far from here. We can drive through and have a look. People know my car; you'll be safe."

"A squatter camp? I don't think so, Jack…"

"Look, we can drive along their road for a little while so you can see what it's like, and then we'll turn and come back to the main road. It'll take maybe fifteen minutes. It's up to you, but I know you're interested in these communities by the questions you've been asking."

He was right about that. I had been pressing Jack to tell me more about any raskols he knew. But all he had offered was that they were not as bad as the media made out. But to drive into one of their camps – it seemed a ridiculous and downright dangerous move.

Jack sensed my reluctance. "If you're worried about some bad blokes jumping us, then you've got nothing to worry about. They're all asleep at this time of day or chewing betel nuts someplace. The last place they'd be waiting is along a road in their own camp. There'd be nothing to steal!" He laughed at his own joke.

Every warning I had read told me to avoid these squatter settlements like the plague. They were the breeding ground of the raskol horde for God's sake. Nevertheless, a dark part of me wanted to see what one looked like with my own eyes. It was like driving past a road accident on the way to work: you couldn't resist a peek. And, so, before I could back out, I nodded, wondering the folly to which I was agreeing.

The squatter camp road we turned onto was potholed and uneven. The far side of the road had a gaping fissure as if subsidence had affected its camber and then simply caved in. No city repairmen came down here, I guessed. As expected, the road and its surrounds looked dirty and litter-infested, more so than the earlier intersection. There were a few people in the vicinity, both men and women, but none of them seemed threatening. They were walking along, chatting and minding their own business. But this wasn't the residential quarter I'd expected; instead, it was an area of disrepair and corrugated fences. It looked like a feeder route into a squatter camp rather than the road through one. I asked Jack about this.

"The camp's up there." He was pointing up to the right. "You can see the backs of the shacks. But everyone here's from the camp."

I looked up, beyond the fencing and bushy palms, at the top halves of shacks that might have been homes. Some were made of wood, others of corrugated metal. Most had tyres or large rocks holding down their roofs. They looked as ramshackle as anywhere in the Third World. I lowered my gaze to a collection of large stone boulders on the other side of the road. They were about the right size for a raskol to smash a car window with, I reckoned. A stray dog lolloped along the cracked excuse for a pavement while another scratched itself in the middle of the road. The mongrel faced no danger of a car hitting it because of the potholes: no vehicle could drive faster than a walking pace.

To say the district looked neglected was an understatement. It seemed as if the authorities had abandoned the place. And yet the further we drove, the more people I could see going about their daily business of traipsing along, spilling red drool from their mouths. An impromptu roadside market had been set up, manned mainly by the lady folk of the settlement. Large ice coolers of cold water bottles sat alongside fruit and vegetables: all laid out on fabric mats. Trade seemed light but was enough for the women to stay for the day.

I asked Jack how many people lived in these so-called squatter camps.

"More than half the city, I reckon. Maybe more. But you can see why the young boys join gangs – there's nothing else for them to do. But not everyone is like that." We drove for a few more metres and then stopped. The road ended at a thin weed-encrusted track. Its well-worn path led up into the surrounding hills. Litter encrusted its edges. We turned the car around and made our way back to the main road. I had survived being as close to a raskol camp as I dared.

14

Jack parked the car in a layby that offered a commanding view of the capital, which from my perch made it look devoid of litter and almost attractive. The main central core, the location of my hotel, was to the left of our position, a juxtaposition of modern high-rises nestled in and around a tropical hillside. In front of that was the ocean, an expanse that only ended with the unseen northern tip of Queensland, some 340 miles distant. But the most interesting aspect of the panorama was a stilt village to my right.

Hanuabada is one of only two stilt villages in Port Moresby; the other I'd seen near the Koki Fish Market. Hanuabada was much bigger, made up of a few hundred individual homes perched on wooden platforms over the ocean connected by wooden walkways. Before World War II, the houses were made from mud-covered timber, covered with traditional thatched roofing, but when a fire destroyed most them during the war, they were upgraded. Instead of thatch they had corrugated iron and instead of soil and tree branches they had prefabricated panelling. The new building materials gave the village an uneven look of modernity mixed with primitive. I asked Jack whether we could see the houses up close.

Jack nodded. "Maybe. We'll have to get permission from the elders."

I hadn't considered this. Maybe I ought to give the stilt village a miss. I didn't fancy the idea of dealing with elders.

Jack was staring down at the village. "But I think we can get permission, but you must let me do all the talking."

The conversation was taking on an unreal air. "How will we meet the elders?"

"We just drive in and meet them."

What if they're out fishing or asleep? I wanted to say but instead asked whether it was safe down there.

"Totally safe. The stilt village isn't like the squatter settlements. The people in the village have been living there for centuries. They were the first people to settle in Port Moresby. That's why the Aussies rebuilt their homes after the fire burned them down. These people are part of our history, mate."

We drove down a winding hill, passing another police car. Its occupants glanced at us as we sped by, but nothing else. And then, ten minutes later, we came to the edge of the stilt village. It was accessible via a strip of road which led down into a dip. We drove into the slope and then parked by a collection of abandoned cars that lay next to a few regular, land-based, shacks. Bedraggled palm trees stooped over them, almost obscuring their verandas and corrugated metal fencing.

Nobody seemed to be about, which I thought was strange. Maybe everyone *was* out fishing. Washing hanging outside the homesteads was the only clue we were not in an abandoned village.

"I'm going to lower the windows so they can see us," intoned Jack. "We'll be stared at but don't react. Just sit and say nothing."

"So there are people here now?"

Jack nodded.

Feeling ominously tense, Jack turned off the engine and lowered the side windows. I suddenly felt very exposed.

15

A naked child, a girl of about six, emerged from one of the homes and watched us. Behind her, a woman swished some clothes aside and regarded us too. From around a corner, a man came. He was bare-chested, chewing betel nut and unsmiling. He had a lot of tattoos that made him look *tribal*. His face was unreadable.

Heeding Jack's instructions, I said nothing as the man approached my window. I tried smiling but I was too tense to produce anything other than a thin grimace. Jack spoke first, and uttered one word: "Damena."

The man studied Jack and then his face relaxed slightly. "Damena?"

"Damena."

I wondered what damena meant but didn't think it was the right time to ask for a lesson in the local dialect. And then Jack and the villager were talking in full sentences, none of which I could understand. It was a thorough conversation, involving nodding, some thoughtful frowns and plenty of eyeballing at me. Finally, Jack turned to me. I fully expected him to say: I'm sorry, Jason, but this man is going to cook you in a pot with some carrots. Please leave the vehicle in an orderly manner. Instead, he said, "He says we need to get out and speak to the chief."

Jesus! Speak to the chief? Was that good or bad? It didn't sound good to me. In films, whenever someone has to speak to the chief, they usually ended up in a pot. I didn't get a chance to ask for clarification because Jack was already climbing out of the car. I jumped out, too, into stifling heat of a sultry Papuan afternoon. Mr Tattoo led us around the corner where a sight to behold waited: another bare-chested man standing with a huge machete. He was with two other men. They had machetes as well. Behind the trio was a wooden table and behind the table were the stilt houses. All three men glared at us and so we stopped in our tracks. I felt my testicles shrivel in alarm. A few curious children, peered from wooden porches, spying on the shenanigans going on in their midst.

"Say nothing," Jack whispered my way. "This is the elder."

I nodded and held my breath. This chief was in his late fifties, I guessed, and lean as hell. He had short, bubbly grey hair and keen eyes. It was the knife that was giving me the jitters though. Why was he standing there with a large machete? What had they been doing with it? While I wondered whether to make a run for it, the chief conferred with Mr Tattoo for a few moments, then walked over to us, studying Jack and then me. After a tense few seconds, Jack was interrogated, with the chief asking all the questions and occasionally stealing glances my way. Finally, the chief nodded and then smiled. His hard features softened in the space of a half-second. Jack turned to me. "The chief says you're welcome to see his village, and you have his permission to look at the houses, as long as you don't go inside any or take any photographs."

I gushed a smile at the man. He had spared me! The relief was enormous. And while I breathed easily for the first time in a good while, everyone shook hands and I thanked the chief again. It was only then that I noticed what was on the wooden table behind him: half a dozen frankfurter sausages. It appeared we had interrupted the stilt village's barbeque preparation.

The chief summoned a teenage boy, his son, he told me via Jack. He would be my guide. The boy seemed pleased with his new and unexpected role and eagerly led me past the chief and his advisors towards the elevated wooden boardwalk on stilts. Jack stayed behind to chat with the men.

"This is house," the boy uttered, stating the obvious as he pointed at one. I nodded eagerly as if I were under the tutelage of a master architect. A child's face peered from the doorway. When I waved, the face was gone. The house was like all the rest: an uncomplicated one-storey structure with slatted, open-air windows and a simple door. It rested on a wooden platform supported by sturdy sections of tree trunks. Other homes had rubber tyres hanging on their outside walls; buoyancy aids should a child fall in, I supposed. Wooden ladders offered access to the ocean, which at this time was just estuarine mud. The teenager suggested that crabs could be caught down there, which explained the dozen or so people in the middle of the harbour, bending into the shallows.

The boy asked where I was from and when I told him he smiled. "I know England! It's where Manchester United is? You know Manchester United?"

I nodded, telling him I lived in a town close to Manchester.

"You live in Manchester United?"

"No, just near it."

"You are lucky."

We walked back to where Jack and the others were. Once again, I thanked everyone for their hospitality and then stood awkwardly while the villagers nodded and smiled. As Jack and I headed back to the car, I asked Jack what he'd said upon the first encounter with a villager, when he'd said 'damena' over and over.

"It means salt in our language. When the bloke came over, I recognised his features were the same as mine; I knew we were both part of the Motu tribe. So I was saying that we were from the same salt; that we were one and the same. That made it easier to see the chief."

16

As night settled over Port Moresby, I was safely ensconced in my hotel again, enjoying an expensive meal and a cooling South Pacific Export beer. Outside, raskols might be running loose, causing madness and mayhem, but inside my maximum security hotel, guarded by armed protection personnel and 24-hour CCTV operation, I felt as safe as could be. Before arriving in Port Moresby, I honestly believed that the only local people I would meet were raskols or people up to no good. How wrong that notion turned out; people had welcomed me wherever I had gone. And to think I wanted to delete the country from my itinerary, believing it a little too dangerous for a traveller like me. Well, what a mistake that would have been. In the end, I had thoroughly enjoyed myself in a nation shunned by most tourists.

But it was almost time to move on; the next day I was carrying on with my journey around the Pacific, this time to a country called the Solomon Islands.

Top L-R: *View of downtown Port Moresby taken from my hotel (note the car park – where an Australian man was shot in the buttock); A woman wandering to the Koki Fish Market*
Middle L-R: *Me looking brave in Papua New Guinea; Hanuabada stilt village, home to machete-wielding men; St Mary's Catholic Church, one of the oldest in the city*
Bottom: L-R: *Parliament Building; Port Moresby street scene*

Chapter 2. Honiara, Solomon Islands

Interesting fact: The Solomon Islands is made up of over 900 individual islands.

I knew almost nothing about the Solomon Islands. All I knew was they had seen some major fighting during World War II, and that was it. Zilch. Nothing else. Thankfully, the in-flight magazine offered some facts for me to savour.

The article said that, although English was the official language of the Solomon Islands, less than 5% of the population spoke it fluently. Another interesting piece of information told me about the name of the country. Apparently, in the Sixteenth century, a bearded Spanish explorer called Alvaro de Mendaña found himself the first European to set eyes on the tropical islands.

After making landfall near what is now the capital, Honiara, Mendaña and his men discovered a rich deposit of gold in a nearby river. The Spaniard captain declared the find a miracle and told his crew that the gold was the mysterious source of King Solomon's wealth. Some of his crewmembers might have doubted this miraculous verdict – after all, they were thousands of miles from Solomon's Middle Eastern kingdom, and, besides, other, far richer, gold deposits had been found all over the world – but they all kept quiet not wanting to upset the captain. And so, for no logical reason whatsoever, Mendaña decreed he had found the fabled mines of the old Hebrew king and scribed the name Islas Salomón on his newly made map.

At just after noon, following a two-hour flight, we began our descent over a rainy mass of land called Guadalcanal, the main island of the Solomon's. Like Papua New Guinea, Guadalcanal's coastal plains were flat expanses of dense rainforest mixed with sporadic inlets, but I had little time to consider this because, a few minutes later, we were down on the runway, fat raindrops splattering the windows and obscuring the view. But I did not care a jot: I was in the second country of the Pacific tour.

It was still raining when I jumped in an airport taxi. Water coated the front windscreen, its wipers swishing back and forth to little effect. It was like we were in a car wash. "We'll have to pull over," said the driver, an affable dark-skinned man with an improbable mop of frizzy blonde-ginger hair. It was as if he had dyed it, but I knew he hadn't; his hair was completely natural, a common trait among Solomon Islanders. We stopped by the side of the road. "I'll wait for the rain to ease, I think."

His hair was amazing. I wanted to touch it but restrained myself in case he considered me a psychopath. Solomon Islanders' hair is famous across the region and has puzzled scientists for years. Many used to believe that the prevalence of blonde hair (up to ten percent of the local population) was the result of European missionaries and explorers infecting the gene pool. This was a reasonable assumption; after all, the only other place on Earth where naturally occurring blonde hair was common was in Northern Europe. But in 2003, this theory was proved wrong by a bunch of clever people who arrived in the Solomon Islands with DNA testing kits. They asked a large number of islanders to spit into test tubes and then took the samples away. When the results came in, they were astounded. Instead of finding the European blonde hair variant, they discovered a brand new one; one they had never seen before. Somehow, and nobody knows why, blonde hair in the Solomon Islands arose naturally and independently, the only place outside of Europe to do so.

Anyway, while I had been privately studying the man's hair, the rain eased sufficiently to allow us passage. We turned right and hit the Kukum Highway, a grand name for what turned out to be the road from hell.

2

The Kukum Highway is the main (and sometimes only) route in the Solomon Islands. It traverses the Northern edge of Guadalcanal Island, passing through the capital, Honiara, as it follows the curve of the coast. Being the main road, I assumed it would be of good quality. It wasn't. The Kukum Highway was one of the worst roads upon which I have ever travelled.

Unlike its name suggested, the highway was a simple dual carriageway with a surface resembling the moon. Potholes and craters covered fifty percent of the road, meaning that traffic had to go slower than a walking speed. Trucks, buses, cars and taxis all had to drive at ridiculously slow speeds or else risk significant damage to their undersides. As soon as we joined the jam, pedestrians left us in their wake. An old woman in a floppy hat passed us like she was a sprinter. Without warning, our left front wheel sloshed into a pothole puddle; something banged and then scraped. The taxi driver didn't seem overly concerned at the battering his taxi was taking, and neither did anyone else: the people of the Solomon Islands were taking the lunacy of the Kukum Highway in their stride.

"Bad potholes," I said.

"Yeah," the driver agreed.

We rumbled to a complete stop in a gridlock of traffic. Ahead was a truck which was trying to negotiate the biggest pothole so far. It was such a crater that the truck had to go onto the other side of the road, blocking up everything in both directions. It was insane that the government had allowed things to deteriorate to such a degree. How could trade function properly when it took so long for anything to be delivered?

"So no one fixes them?" I asked.

The man shrugged. "Sometimes they fill them with stones but as soon as it rains, they get washed out. They've been like this for years and keep getting worse. I've heard the Japanese are coming to fix the highway, but I don't know if that's true."

The lorry moved on, and so did we. In the end, it took almost two hours to travel 7.5 miles. Under normal circumstances, it would have taken ten minutes.

3

The Coral Sea Resort & Casino was positioned on a nice slice of Solomon Island coastline. As well as a casino, it had nests of palm trees, a little wedge of sand, a deck for viewing the sunset and the possibility of being snatched by a saltwater crocodile.

Like Northern Australia and Papua New Guinea, the Solomon Islands are home to these giant reptiles. In 2017, there were ten crocodile attacks on people in the country and many more attacks on livestock. The attacks were so worrying that the police assembled a special crack unit called the Crocodile Control Team. Armed with rifles and torches, the crack croc cops (say that three times!) had to wait until sunset before heading into the mangroves in a banana boat. Why they had to use a banana boat and not a regular boat was unclear. However, their mode of transport seemed to work because one of their first kills was a 21-foot brute that may have been responsible for the death of a six-year-old village boy. The youngster had been swimming with some pals in a local creek when a crocodile grabbed him. The same crocodile might have eaten a 20-year-old man the month before that.

After checking into my room, I wandered down to the Coral Sea, keeping my distance from the edge of the water. I was in the hotel grounds, but there was no one around, except for a barman in the distance polishing glasses. If I were grabbed, nobody would know. This part of the Coral Sea was not mangrove, and so I doubted any monsters were lurking, but it was best to be safe than sorry. It made me recall a horrific story from Australia. A 34-year-old man had been fishing when a crocodile sprang out of the water and seized his left leg. He grabbed a tree trunk as the reptile tried to drag him down to the mangrove. The crocodile attempted to break the man's grip by swishing its tail and rolling over. This did the trick because the man's knees popped out of their joints like matchsticks and the fisherman let go of the tree trunk.

At this point, the man, Todd Bairstow, thought he was a goner and took one last gulp of air before he hit the swampy water. And then he discovered, much to his astonishment, that the water was not deep enough for the crocodile to drown him in. With a renewed surge of hope, Mr Bairstow began a fight for his life, adrenalin pumping like mad through his body.

With the crocodile twisting him into the mud, Bairstow gouged at its eyes with his fingers and then, when it briefly let go of his leg, he stuck his arm into the crocodile's mouth and jabbed at a flap of tissue called the palatal valve. This fleshy membrane in a reptile's throat stops water from getting into its oesophagus while underwater. The ploy worked and the crocodile let go. And then, despite a bleeding leg and lacerated arm, Bairstow crawled up the bank and grasped hold of the tree trunk again. When he looked down, he noticed the crocodile chomping on something else. Inexplicably, he realised it was his feet, an impossible situation given the distance involved. Then the horrible realisation hit Bairstow: his legs had stretched with just skin holding them together. His legs were so long it seemed as if he was made from rubber.

With all the screaming and thrashing going on, help arrived. A man from a nearby bar rushed down to the river and whacked the green beast with rocks and sticks. Finally, the crocodile gave up and left. As for Bairstow, he survived the attack but needed five months of corrective surgery where, unbelievably, he got the use of his legs back. Doctors had to amputate one of his fingers, though. Later, when he was told his assailant had been captured and taken to a commercial crocodile farm, he went to see it. "I visited the bastard and threw it a chicken," he said of the encounter, showing he bore no grudges.

As for me, I decided to go and see a little bit of Honiara.

4

I walked east along the ridiculousness of the Kukum Highway, the traffic grinding ponderously along because of the potholes. A row of shops was to my right, all run-down and lacking lustre. To my left, towards the ocean, the sight was better. The presence of palm trees, no matter how spindly or bedraggled, always provoked a feeling of wellbeing in me. Perhaps it was because I spent most of my formative years in dismal England, a place devoid of anything remotely tropical. Or maybe it was because I liked the frilly and floppy fronds. Whatever it was, the sight of them, juxtaposed with the Pacific Ocean, made me content.

Another thing that pleased me was I felt completely safe. Though I was the only white guy in town (as far as I could tell), no one was casting looks at me which suggested malice. No one seemed curious as to my passage. Even the car number plates made me feel welcome: *Solomon Islands*, each one decreed, *The Hapi Isles*.

Honiara hasn't always been a place to smile about. In fact, tourist numbers are still shockingly low and have been ever since the riots of 2006. That year saw the election of a new prime minister who, many islanders believed, had rigged the vote with help from Chinese businessmen. Uprisings began, especially in Honiara's Chinatown district, and shops and businesses were looted or burnt down. An Australian military contingent arrived and restored peace. While they patrolled the streets, the new prime minister resigned, the Chinese left and the few tourists who had been coming to the Solomon Islands stopped altogether.

I passed a trio of bushy blonde-haired women waiting at a bus stop. They looked at me, all of them smiling. "You Aussie?" one of them said.

"No, English."

"English? We don't get many English people here. You lost?" All three laughed good-naturedly at this, and I did too. But she was correct about the lack of English people. According to the latest figures from 2015, only 387 British passport holders visited the Solomon Islands that year, the least visited country by Brits of all the places I'd be going. Even Antarctica received ten times as many British visitors.

Further along, I stopped to take in the view of downtown Honiara. As an urban area, it stretched out along the Kukum Highway, east to west. No one in their right mind would ever call it a pretty town. The capital of the Solomon Islands was a dishevelled place, where tropically-stained buildings and cracked pavements were the norms. I could have been in the back streets of Ghana or Guatemala; nothing stood out as being remarkable or even memorable. Hardware shops, cheap eateries and general stores made up most of the high street. Nescafe sighs abounded as did top-up advertisements for Vodafone. One store, a vivid blue establishment called Ma's Shopping caught my eye. Although I could not see into its darkened interior, I knew what it sold because the owners had painted pictures of the wares onto the blue exterior background. Jeans, skirts, T-shirts, shoes, bags, hairdryers and, very specifically, make-up brushes were for sale. Behind the shops, rolling green hills filled the view, the most picturesque aspect of my current vista, but even this higher ground did not invite further exploration and so I headed back to the hotel so I could plan a proper sightseeing trip the next day.

5

It was evening time and since I was staying in a ground-floor room, I sprayed mosquito repellent over myself before I pored over the map of Honiara. Tourist sites were thin on the ground, I quickly discovered. There was the Central Market, which I thought sounded interesting. And there was a museum, which, in the absence of much else, might be worth a visit. There was something called the Solomon Scouts and Coastwatchers Monument, which, ordinarily would not have made it into any top ten city attractions, and yet did in Honiara; so I circled that on my map. Then there was a church and the port, and that was it. I would try to see them all the next morning and then, in the afternoon, maybe hire a taxi to take me to some war memorials up in the hills.

That settled, I went to the hotel restaurant and then the bar. After swatting away a mosquito, I ordered a beer and sat down on a stool at the front. Not long after, a Westerner, a man in his late forties, entered the bar and we got chatting. He was Australian and worked in Honiara as a technical advisor to a bank.

"It's the pits, living here," he told me over a SolBrew. "Nothing to do except work. The weekends are dull unless you enjoy sitting on a fly-infested beach. The supermarkets are shit. The restaurants are worse. The highlight of my day is sitting in this bar or the one up at the King Solomon. If you've not been there yet, try one of their pizzas."

I asked him how long he had lived in the Solomon Islands.

"This is my second year. At the end of this year, I'm out of here. Back to Sydney. Can't wait. The only reason I'm here is the package, mate." He briefly let go of his beer bottle to rub his forefinger and thumb together. "I get a house and car, plus a salary you wouldn't believe. But I earn every cent."

I asked him whether he liked anything about Honiara.

"The ocean's cool. But that's about it." He took a large slurp of his beer. He almost drained the rest of the bottle in one go. "But the worst thing about living here, apart from the boredom, is the smelly people. I don't know whether it's because they're naturally smelly or because they don't have access to showers, but they whiff like mad. But I'm the only one who seems to notice, so maybe it's me."

I took a sip of my SolBrew. It really was rather nice. "Is it safe to walk around town? I'm planning on having a wander tomorrow."

"No problem. Just don't flash the cash or make it too obvious you're a tourist. And if you come across a betel nut chewer – and you will – be a bit more wary of him. But you'll be fine, apart from the fact you'll be bored out of your mind. I can't think of a single thing you'd want to see."

I listed the things I'd circled on my map.

The guy actually laughed. "The Scout Monument? Really? I don't want to spoil it for you, but I hope you're not expecting much. As for the museum, I've only been once and it was closed."

I drained my bottle of beer and bid the man who hated Honiara farewell.

6

The next morning was bright and sunny, always the best type of day for sightseeing, unless I was in the tropics, which I was. After liberally dousing myself in factor-50 sunscreen, I donned my hat and sunglasses and headed onto the main street again.

Within five minutes I was sweating like a man who should be in a hospital, but knowing this would happen, I had brought a flannel, which I kept using on my forehead and chest. The latter involved surreptitiously lifting my T-shirt and rubbing the moisture away before anyone noticed.

A betel nut chewer noticed, though. His middle-aged lips were slick with red and yet he looked a little bit disgusted with me. But who could blame him, for I had given him a full side view of my portly, sweat-lathered belly? I passed him quickly and moved on, coming to the Office of the Prime Minister and Cabinet, a large and long blue building that resembled a 1970s secondary school. I couldn't see any dignitaries and so crossed the road towards the Solomon Island's National Museum. Inside its grounds, I found a collection of large thatched-roofed buildings. All of them were locked. Even so, I wandered around in the hope that a museum curator might see me and open up something. No one did, and so as a consolation I took a photo of some large wooden figures that looked tribal. Then I stood around for a full minute, wondering what to do next. Then I left.

I walked further into town, seeing that the Scout Monument was next on my list. I found it five minutes away and discovered it better than the Aussie banker had suggested it would be. True, it wasn't the most magnificent monument in the world, but neither was it the worst. But, in a city devoid of other such things, it could confidently claim to be one of the most splendid statues in the Solomon Islands.

The Solomon Scouts and Coastwatchers Monument depicted four bronze figures on a sturdy white plinth. One of the men was staring northwards through binoculars while another man sat hunched over a communication device, speaking earnestly into a handset. A third man, armed with a rifle, sat behind him, while the fourth pointed at something in the sea.

The Solomon Scouts had nothing to do with Robert Baden-Powell's troop of young campers but were instead a well-trained team of local islanders (the Scouts), who assisted a handful of Australian and Europeans (the Coastwatchers) in spotting Japanese activity along the coast. Whenever they noticed anything, they would contact the Australian navy.

On one occasion in 1943, a Coastwatcher happened to be looking at just the right place at just the right time. The eagle-eyed gent saw a Japanese destroyer ram an American patrol boat. Quickly, two Solomon Scouts set out to sea in a canoe to find wreckage or survivors.

Over at the scene of the collision, a dozen or so American servicemen suddenly found themselves in the ocean without a boat. With two crew members dead and another severely burned, the group swam through shark-infested waters for four hours until they reached a deserted island. Cruelly, they found it devoid of food and drinking water. After a suitable rest, they had no choice but to swim a further five hours to another island in the distance. Thankfully on this island they found fresh coconuts and a river. And while they were recuperating, they noticed a tiny canoe coming towards them. Inside it were the Solomon Scouts who had set off half a day earlier. After the scouts handed over some yams and cigarettes, the American officer in charge found a coconut husk and scrawled a message for the scouts to take back to Honiara, signing his name: Lieutenant John Fitzgerald Kennedy, future President of the United States. Six days later, rescuers arrived and newspapers around the world went crazy for the story, mainly because the American lieutenant at the heart of the story was the son of a prominent businessman and politician.

Kennedy never forgot about the Solomon Scouts. He partly paid for each of them to have a new house built and later, when he became President, invited them to attend his inauguration. It was at this point that events turned a little sour. When the scouts arrived at Honiara Airport for their flight to Washington, officials refused to let them board the plane, citing their poor clothes and poor language skills as enough reason. They told the scouts that they would be an embarrassment to the country. Instead, two upstanding Solomon Island representatives took their seats and attended the inauguration in their place.

I stared up at the monument that lay in the middle of a chaotic and dusty street in Honiara. No one except me was looking at it; everyone else was passing without a second glance. And though it did not look awe-inspiring or massive in size, it was a fitting memorial to those two men (and others like them) who had risked their lives in the treacherous waters around the Solomon Islands.

7

Around the corner from the Solomon Scouts and Coastwatchers Monument was Honiara's port area. It was a buzzing place of activity, mainly involving platoons of young men passing boxes to each other until the supplies reached a ship. If they weren't doing that, they were heaving on thick coils of rope. Everywhere I looked there was unloading and loading, coiling and knotting: I could not recall seeing such a hard-working port area in my life.

The smell along the jetty was ripe, though. As I moved along the edge of the oily water, the smell got worse until I found the culprit: an overflowing industrial-sized bin that no one had emptied in a long while.

There was a public notice near it that had a list of prohibited activities and fines. Chewing or spitting betel nut would incur a penalty of fifty Solomon dollars (£5); drinking alcohol, prostitution and illegal marketing was the same. The lowest fine was for dropping litter, where an offender could expect to part with twenty dollars if caught. Judging by the amount on the floor, I guessed the fines were not enforced often.

I left the port and headed to the Central Market, a focus of fruit, flowers and fish, offered by the thousand or so individual vendors. It was heaving with shoppers, mostly women. Laid out on large sheets of blue plastic tarpaulin were watermelons, yams, coconuts, eggplant, mangoes, bananas, pineapples, sweet potatoes and oranges. From bulging white sacks, green leafy things spilled. Sitting around the produce, either on upturned plastic buckets or cheap plastic chairs were the vendors. For once, the smell was refreshing.

"Hey, mista," shouted a woman. "You wanna buy or are ya' just lookin'?"

The buxom, dark-haired lady was about forty and presided over a floor space of peanuts.

I glanced down. "Sorry, just looking." She was already eying other customers.

Honiara's Central Market was the biggest source of fresh food in the country. But with that, came a few problems, not least of which was crime. With security so weak, the vendors often resorted to sleeping overnight in the market, making sure no one stole any of their wares. Another problem was the people trying to sell *kwaso*, an illegally distilled homebrew made from fruit cordial, sugar and yeast. It was so potent that people died drinking the stuff. The third issue the market faced was linked to the fee each vendor had to pay when renting their selling space. It wasn't a fair system traders said, because, instead of being based upon the *amount* of produce sold, the rent was based on the *variety* of food on offer. So, if one vendor brought a hundred bags of potatoes to the market, she paid the same fee as the woman who brought three small baskets of them. But for the trader who brought one small bag of coconuts and one small bag of peanuts, she would pay more than them both.

I wandered through the stalls, nudging shoulders with the shoppers out to grab a bargain. The crowd more or less jostled me through, but it was all good-natured. Even with the unfairness of rent allocation, the vendors seemed a happy bunch, especially with the full-on trading going on. Outside, at the rear of the market, I found a foul-smelling area near the water's edge. The odour was from old and rotten fish, remnants from the early morning fish sales. With the boom time over, eight or nine small boats were up on the ramp-like jetty, abandoned until later that evening when they would make the journey back to the commercial fishing boats to fill their ice coolers.

Out in the harbour were the rusted hulls of two ships. They were so close to the jetty that I could have jumped onto them. The smallest of the pair was listing, partly submerged in the shallows; its remains skeletal and brown. It was an eyesore and quite probably an environmental and shipping hazard, too. The other wreck was more substantial and seemed in better condition, though this was relative. It had a gaping wound in its hull and sore-like rust spots everywhere else. It, too, was tilting in the shallow water, but at least it still had streaks of blue paint remaining.

While I stood pondering how the two ships had ended up like this, a man wandered over. He was about my age, but like the ship, not in good health, stick-thin with his chest bones showing. He was chewing away on an ungodly mixture of betel nut and saliva. His red mouth and wiry eyes gave him the look of a madman. One of his cheeks bulged like a hamster's: full to brimming with betel nut.

"Looking at the wrecks?" the man said in surprisingly coherent English.

"Yeah."

The man said nothing; just noisily chewed away next to me.

"How did they get here?" I asked to break the awful sound.

"Tsunami a few years ago." He completed a thoughtful chew. "Maybe five years, or maybe before that, I forget. But these ships got broke and nobody wanted to clean 'em up. Kids sometimes play daredevil games on 'em."

We both stared at the broken boats, considering them in silence and slurp. And then I decided I had one more thing to see before going for lunch. I said goodbye the man and left the market area in search of a church.

8

Honiara's Holy Cross Church stands on a slight hill in the centre of town. The exterior seems rather mundane, consisting of a triangular-shaped entrance with a large cross incorporated into a stained-glass frontage. But what is significant about the Holy Cross Church is its location. The church supposedly sits on the hill that Spaniard Alvaro de Mendaña climbed when he first arrived in the Solomon Islands in 1568.

Mendaña was a staunch Catholic and his reason for exploration, apart from seeking out gold, was to convert any heathens he came across. After he'd planted a cross on the hill, he set out to do this, and his method was simple: his men would turn up at a village and give the locals two choices: one, convert to the Pope's way of thinking or, two, be killed. Most chose the former and became God-fearing Christians. Once Mendaña had enough converts, he made them farm the land and tend livestock. And this was okay for a while in the Solomon Islands until the livestock started running out and the locals had to come up with Plan B.

After convening in a huddle, the islanders nodded grimly and went to work, eventually presenting the Spanish with an alternative meat. When Mendaña scrutinised the offering, he was horrified to discover it was a carefully butchered quarter of a child. After yelling a bit and pushing a few locals to the ground, he decided to abandon his fly-infested settlement. The child was the last straw. For a while, his crew had been ravaged by terrible diseases, which Mendaña himself suffered from. As the ship prepared for departure, Mendaña's fever took a turn for the worse. He died shortly afterwards and his men left without him. Following their retreat, Dutch, English and French ships tried their luck, but hostile locals sent them all packing. It would take three hundred years for a European power to finally lay claim to the Solomon Islands.

I climbed the steps up the hill, glancing at restoration work going on around what looked like a Spanish galleon, perhaps a copy of the one in which Alvaro de Mendaña had arrived. It was surprisingly small and, if the ship was a life-sized reproduction of the vessel that had traversed the Pacific Ocean, then Mendaña and his crew must have been insane. To travel thousands of miles in something that tiny were the actions of the unhinged.

There was service going on inside the church, which surprised me as it was a weekday afternoon. The quarter-full congregation was listening to a white-robed minister reading from a Bible. I turned around and regarded Honiara from my slightly lofty perch. A layer of airborne dust, or maybe car fumes, hung over certain stretches of the broken and bruised Kukum Highway. But the people of Honiara seemed immune to the dirt and the incessant beeping as they made their way into the centre of town. Schoolgirls in burgundy skirts and pale blue shirts, ladies with blonde-ginger hair walking under the shade of multi-coloured sun parasols, businessmen plodding along with ill-fitting suits and trainers and teenage boys in sleeveless T-shirts, shorts and flip-flops, all of them going about their business while I went about mine.

9

After lunch, I asked the hotel to organise a driver for me. I wanted to see the American and Japanese war memorials up in the hills behind Honiara. My driver was called Alwin, a heavyset man in his late twenties with blondish, curly hair. He wasn't chewing betel nut, but I could tell he was partial to it: his teeth were stained red. It was a horrible look, reminding me of a lion that has just eaten a savannah kill.

"We'll go to the American one first, then the Japanese one," he told me. "That's the easiest way to do them."

Alwin loved country and western music. As soon as we set off in his taxi, his CD player was switched on and the mournful melody of a man singing about lost love, accompanied by pedal steel guitars, filled the car. As we trundled on the potholed highway, he hummed along tunelessly until I asked him whether he enjoyed living in the Solomon Islands.

Alwin stared ahead for a few moments, absently negotiating a shallow pothole. I wondered whether he hadn't heard me and was about to repeat the question but he finally answered. "Yeah, I do."

I waited for more insight but when none came, I asked him why.

Again, Alwin seemed in deep thought, or perhaps trying to savour the dulcet tones of Kenny Rogers singing about four hungry children and crops in his fields. "I like the sunny weather – unless we get a cyclone – and I like the ocean. I like my job that pays the rent and I like betel nut. I like it more than booze. I'd be chewing right now if I wasn't working."

Alwin told me that he'd started chewing betel nuts when he was twelve years old. "All my friends were doing it, and my mother didn't seem bothered – she chewed them all the time – and so I tried some. I got a nut wrapped in a leaf and put it in my mouth. One of my mates told me to bite it until it cracked so the juices could come out. Then he told me to shove the whole lot over to the side of my cheek near my gums. That's how I've done it ever since."

"How long do you keep it in your mouth?"

"Maybe twenty, thirty minutes."

We were passing the museum I had visited earlier. It still looked closed. I asked Alwin what betel nut tasted like.

"When I first tried it, it was nasty – real bitter, like eating the end of a pencil. But my mouth started to go numb – a bit like when you're at the dentist – then I started to feel real good, psyched up, you know, lots of energy. I loved it. And before long, I was chewing all the time. The taste didn't bother me after a while."

"Do people get addicted to it, as they do with booze?'

"No!" Alwin shook his head in emphasis. "You can't get addicted to betel nut."

He was possibly wrong about that. But even if he wasn't, the long-term effects of betel nut chewing were disturbing. As well as causing a plethora of nasty complaints such as diarrhoea, shortness of breath, gum disease and the ever-present red teeth, it was likely a cause of oral cancer. In Taiwan, another great betel nut chewing nation, incidents of oral cancer are spiking. Scientists believe the culprit is the betel nut. For this reason, many countries have banned it, including Australia, the UAE and India.

Suddenly, Alwin seemed to have a thought. "You wanna try some?"

I shook my head. "Thanks, but I think I'll stick to SolBrew."

"You sure? I can get some near here. I know all the best places. My brother even grows betel nut trees in his garden."

"I think I'm fine."

"Well if you change your mind…"

We turned away from the highway, heading uphill towards the American War Memorial.

10

The Solomon Islands saw some of the heaviest fighting of World War II. After the Japanese took control of Thailand, the Philippines,

Burma, Malaysia, Singapore and the Dutch East Indies (now Indonesia), they set their sights on the Pacific islands of Papua New Guinea, Fiji, Nauru, Samoa and the Solomon Islands. If they took these nations, they would effectively cut off Australia and the United States.

For six dreadful months between 1942 and 1943, sixty thousand allied troops battled thirty thousand Japanese invaders on the land, sea and air around Guadalcanal, the Solomon's main island. The ground was blown up, pummelled, set on fire and raked with bullets. In the Coral Sea, so many ships were sunk that Honiara's harbour became known as Ironbottom Sound. By the time the Americans drove the Japanese out, seven thousand of their troops were dead together with twenty thousand Japanese. Both sides lost hundreds of aircraft and numerous ships. The battle was such a drain on Japan that it became one of the significant factors that led to its surrender in 1945. And because of the deaths, both countries eventually built memorials to its lost servicemen. After five minutes of travelling uphill, we arrived at the American one.

Abruptly, the country and western tune turned silent when Alwin switched off the car engine. The American War Monument was called the Solomon Island's Peace Park Memorial and stood at the top of a hill, guarded by a sturdy metal fence that discouraged climbing due to the pointy spires that tapered into vicious spikes. Alwin and I climbed out of the car as a kindly local man emerged from a guard post inside the fence. After looking us over, and conversing with Alwin for a moment, the gentleman unlocked the gate and allowed us entry.

The American memorial was well kept and clean. Two huge flags billowed at one end of the surprisingly large complex: one, the American stars and stripes, the other, the green, yellow and blue of the Solomon Islands. In front of the flags were a series of brown marble tablets inscribed with the details of various battles the island had suffered through. I stopped by one tablet. It read: *May this memorial endure the ravages of time until wind, rain and tropical storms wear away its face but never its memories.*

It is more or less impossible to comprehend the scale of death represented at such monuments. It is also hard to imagine the fighting that led to the monument's creation, especially on a sunny day surrounded by the natural environment of the Solomon Islands. The only time I had ever felt any awareness – and it was only slight – about the scale of death a war can produce was when I was twelve. Together with a bunch of classmates, I had taken a school trip to Northern France, and part of the excursion was to visit the mass graves of British troops killed during the Normandy Landings, an event which would take place eighteen months after the fighting in the Solomon Islands. As I had wandered along row upon row of white crosses, most inscribed with a name and age, I began to feel something like sorrow, especially when I looked around and saw thousands more just like them. And that graveyard was only one of many in Northern France dedicated to servicemen who had died.

I walked past the flags and stared down at Honiara. In the distance, snaking its way to the Pacific Ocean was the Mataniko River, a dirty place of warehouses and commercial properties. It was in that river mouth where Mendaña's men had found the supposed trove of Solomon's gold and where, during World War II, thousands of American and Japanese troops had lost their lives. Further inland, sporadic, low-rise tin-roofed homes surrounded by jungle were the only things of interest. All of them stood on wooden stilts. I stared down at the ocean. It was busy with half a dozen or so ships that floated above Ironbottom Sound, the graveyard of the old war boats. From up here, away from the grime and noise, Honiara looked at peace.

11

Only six kilometres separate the American and Japanese War Memorials and yet the journey took thirty minutes due to the potholes that plagued the thin upland road. All the way, I was subjected to yet more country and western music.

"I didn't know people from the Solomon Islands would like this type of music," I eventually said.

"Why?"

It was a fair enough question and one I had no answer for. Why shouldn't someone from the South Pacific enjoy country and western music? It was the same as asking someone from Brazil or India why they liked heavy metal music. It was because they did, simple as that. "No reason, I was just wondering."

"Well, I got into country music because it was the only CD in the car when I bought it. I gave it a spin and didn't really get it, but after playing it over and over, I ended up loving it. My sister loves it too. You want to know my favourite tune?"

I nodded.

"*Friends in Low Places*. You heard of it?"

I shook my head.

He turned off the CD player and began to sing. It was a tuneless version of whatever song was his favourite but I had no clue whether I'd heard it or not. "Who's it by?"

"Garth Brooks. Ever heard of him?"

I nodded. Garth Brooks was one of the most popular country and western stars in America. I thought everyone had heard of him. Alwin switched on the CD player again and skipped a few tracks. And then his favourite song came on which, to a non-connoisseur, sounded just like all the other songs: jangly minor chords, pedal steel guitars, curled-vowel vocals and even a fiddle. But for Alwin, it set forth a new bout of crooning, one which made me smile. I was just thankful that we eventually arrived at the top of another hill so the music could cease.

The Japanese Memorial was locked up tight, but instead of a metal fence, a tall, white-painted stone wall surrounded it. Unlike the American one, I had to pay to get inside, handing over a $10 Solomon note (£1) to an old man wearing flip-flops and an orange high visibility vest that claimed he was Safeguard Security. How effective he would be against insurgents hell-bent on destruction was up for debate.

Since Alwin had never visited the Japanese memorial, he was eager to see inside, too, and thus I paid for him as well. We both walked inside and read the inscription beyond the entrance. In Japanese and English, it said the monument was in honour of and to give respect to both the Japanese and Americans who had given up their precious lives during the war. It also offered thanks to the Solomon Island's government for allowing Japan to build the monument in the first place, a monument erected by ex-Japanese servicemen who returned to the island in 1980 for that purpose.

It was smaller than the American memorial across the valley but no less impressive. While Alwin busied himself taking a photo of the main section which consisted of two tall marble pillars, I was drawn to a large bronze statue of a heroically posed man.

The placard told me the statue had been cast in the 1930s by a man called Eikichi Takahashi. He called it the *Sound of the Tide*. He was greatly honoured when his hometown of Ishinomaki placed it a prominent position by the sea. But then war broke out and Takahashi abandoned his art and joined the army.

After training, he was sent to the Solomon Islands where he was killed in action soon after arriving. Just like that, dead and gone in a country far from home.

After the war, his hometown and family donated the statue he had made and had it shipped to the Solomon Islands. This statue, above all other facets of both nations' memorials, made it more personal. Here was the name of someone who had died with something he had created.

I joined Alwin at the marble towers. The inscription there read: *At this place repose all the spirits of those who sacrificed their lives in the Second World War.* "I think the American one is better," said Alwin. I thought otherwise; I preferred this one.

12

That evening, I decided to take the advice of the Aussie I'd met in the hotel bar, and wandered up the hill to the King Solomon Hotel, a ten-minute walk away. I wanted to sample some of the hotel's famous pizza. After walking past a monstrosity that called itself the central post office, I turned left along the pleasantly named Hibiscus Avenue, home of the Australian High Commission, and the King Solomon Hotel. The sun was going down over Honiara and the traffic was heading out of the central core into the suburbs.

I had to admit that the entrance to the hotel looked good – a traditional palm-covered roof that towered above a huge wooden carving that might have been a fish or a royal coat of arms, I could not tell. Hanging above the doors was a large sign that read: Welkam. I entered the hotel in search of pizza.

The dimly-lit bar area was already quite busy. Most of the patrons looked Western, with a huddle of men hanging around the bar and a group of four, which included a middle-aged woman, sitting around a table. One western man was by himself, reading something on his phone. I couldn't see the Australian man I'd been speaking to the previous evening anywhere.

I found an empty table and wondered whether any of the ex-pats would invite me over but none even acknowledged my presence. Perhaps the Solomon Island's ex-pat community was so closely-knit that to get in you had to know someone or else be chased by a crocodile up the street. Instead, I cast a glance across the menu and spotted precisely what I wanted: a ham and mushroom pizza, served with a bottle of cold SolBrew.

While I waited for my meal to arrive, I regarded the group of four sitting a few tables away. One of them glanced over; then quickly looked away when he saw me staring. He said something to the others. All of them looked and I smiled and nodded by way of acknowledgement. None of them returned the gesture and, instead, turned away and carried on with their private discussion. Friendly bunch, I thought.

I looked at my phone, just like the man across from me had been doing until his departure. I researched information on Vanuatu, my next port of call. The small Pacific nation was made up of 82 individual islands, of which 65 had people living on them. A lot of the islands had either been made by volcanoes or were volcanoes. I also read that Vanuatu invented bungee jumping.

Every year for the past few centuries, villagers on Pentecost Island have built a thirty-metre tall wooden structure to celebrate the yam harvest. Skilled builders strap it together while keen-eyed villagers scour the area around its base to clear it of rocks. Back in the village, when a party kicks off, a few dozen men and teenage boys will be measured up for the vines. These vines will be their only safety feature when they dive off the structure later on, and so they have to be just the right length: too long, the diver will crash his head into the ground; too short, he might crash into the structure itself.

After some hard partying, the first jumper will climb the structure. At the top, someone will tie his vines around his ankles and connect them to a strong supporting beam. Down below, women will be dancing and men giving pantomimes. And then, when the jumper is given the final nod, he will shuffle to the edge of the platform, cross his arms over his chest and then tuck his head into his shoulders. After checking that his vines are in place, he will throw himself off the sixty-foot perch, headfirst, the same height as a six-storey building. Unlike a regular bungee jumper, though, he will not spring back into the air; instead, he will land on the soft soil with his head and shoulders nudging the surface. That's why the vines have to be so precisely measured.

In recorded history, only two men have died while doing the Vanuatu dive. One was killed when Queen Elizabeth II was watching. Because his jump was undertaken outside of the regular yam harvesting season, the vines attached to the man's ankles were not quite ripe. When he dived off, they failed to arrest his descent and the man ended up breaking his back. He later died in hospital. Needless to say, Prince Philip refused the invitation to jump next.

Speaking of Prince Philip, a tribe on the Vanuatu island of Tanna believe that the Duke of Edinburgh is their God. According to their prophecy, a messiah would appear on their island at some point, and they would know it was him because of the way others acted around him. So when the Queen and Prince Philip arrived on Tanna in 1974 and the locals witnessed first-hand how obsequious every official was towards the pair, together with the lordly way in which Prince Philip conducted himself, they checked the divination and nodded to themselves: their Messiah had shown up.

Prince Philip, totally unaware of this turn of events, returned to Buckingham Palace after his South Pacific Royal tour. Someone told him of the strange islanders in Vanuatu who thought he was the Almighty. After taking this news in, the Prince decided to humour the tribe and sent them a signed photograph of himself. When the tribe received this unexpected gift from their God, they were elated beyond belief. All 30,000 of them. After the elders placed the photograph in a shrine, they sent a gift back to the deity: a traditional club with which they used to batter pigs to death. What the Prince thought of the strange gift is unknown, but he must have thought enough of it because he got a royal photographer to snap off a picture of him posing with the club. When I found this photo online, I couldn't help but smile. There Prince Phillip was, in an expensive and well-tailored suit, holding a long, tapered, swine-killing club. He packaged the photo and sent it to Vanuatu. When the people of Tanna Island received the image, it caused a renewed frenzy. Their God had bestowed another gift! And since then, the people of this small island live in the hope that their Lord will pack a suitcase in Buckingham Palace so that he can come and live among them.

The arrival of my pizza broke my thoughts. It did look good; so maybe the dour Australian man had redeemed himself. But when I cut off a section and put it into my mouth, I realised he was wrong again. The tomato sauce on the pizza was exactly that – tomato sauce from a bottle of ketchup and not the usual tomato puree used on every other pizza in the world. The chef had also smeared the ham and mushrooms with the stuff, creating a piece of artwork that Jackson Pollock may have found alluring. After forcing down another hideous mouthful, I swilled the whole bottle of beer and left the King Solomon Hotel, disappointed that I would now have to order an expensive meal in my hotel.

My journey back was undertaken in almost darkness, the absence of street lighting meant that it was only car headlamps illuminating Honiara. But I didn't care a jot. As I plodded along, avoiding the holes in the pavement, I was smiling. Honiara might not be beautiful, and it might serve horrid pizzas and be full of potholes, but it had still been a worthy second addition to my list of South Pacific nations.

Top L-R: *The Solomon Islands has great car number plates; The potholes of the Kukum Highway*
Middle L-R: *Ma's Shopping – sells make-up brushes; Imaginatively titled SolBrew Lager*
Bottom, L-R: *The Solomon Scouts and Coastwatchers Monument; Rusted shipwreck near the central market; A woman (note the curious blond hair) sits amid her produce at Honiara Central Market*

CHAPTER 3. PORT VILA, VANUATU

Interesting fact: Some islands in Vanuatu have banned junk food.

Unsurprisingly, six out of every ten people who visit Vanuatu are from Australia or New Zealand. The proximity of these countries (it's the same distance as London is to Helsinki), means that, for an Aussie wanting somewhere different from Bali or Fiji, Vanuatu is a viable third option. Most other visitors come from the rest of the Pacific nations, with China sending over a respectable number of tourists too.

The afternoon flight from Honiara took less than two hours, and after a snooze, a snack and a read of the magazine, I was landing on the runway at Port Vila's Bauerfield International Airport, named after an American fighter pilot shot down in the Solomon Islands. As soon as I stepped into the terminal building, I could see that, for the first time on my trip around the Pacific, a country was actively welcoming tourists. Large, tropical posters thanked me for visiting Vanuatu and told me the exciting things I could do.

I could, for instance, enjoy tribal culture; the accompanying photo showed what looked like a Chinese woman holding a local baby. If I tired of that, I could touch the trunk of what the poster claimed was the World's Largest Banyan Tree. Keeping to the arboreal theme, I could zip-line through jungle treetops if I wanted, or else marvel at magnificent volcanoes. It was all a bit better than being mugged by a raskol or breaking an ankle in a pothole.

The baggage carousel was also tourist friendly, especially if the tourist in question was a beer lover like me because in the centre was a gigantic bottle of Tusker Premium Beer, Vanuatu's local brew. The label showed a terrifying wild boar with massive curled tusks, which explained the name of the ale. The country's flag also featured a curved tusk. The reason for all these tusks was that pigs were an integral part of the nation's heritage, especially the ones that grew the long curved tusks. Scientists have taken great delight in studying these particular pigs because they all share one unusual trait: they are hermaphrodite.

Pigs first arrived in Vanuatu around 1600 years ago. They came with early settlers in their canoes. At first, because there were so few of them, coupled with the fact that the pigs were not choosy in their sexual partners, inbreeding occurred. Every now and again, one piglet would pop out with a bizarre mix of male and female sexual organs, both teat and testes. When this happened, the breeder would grow excited because, if the hermaphrodite pig had ovaries, it would soon be growing the ridiculously curving tusks that everyone loved. These intersex pigs became so sought after that whenever one was born, it caused much celebration.

The luggage belt shifting into action brought me out of my musings, and when my bag arrived, I grabbed it and headed outside to get a taxi.

2

Port Vila lies at the southern end of Efate Island, Vanuatu's most populated land mass. For the first time since Brisbane, I saw tourists walking around. Groups of them were on foot along the main street that ran through the town centre, stopping at souvenir shops or reading menus outside cafes. A teenage girl was ambling along by herself, swishing her phone around in an attempt to find some free Wi-Fi. As well as the tourists, there were plenty of locals, most smiling as they made their way past the elaborately fronted Post Office building with its vivid mural of tribal people cavorting with tropical fish.

In 2016, Vanuatu came out at a very respectable fourth place in a global ranking of happiness, only losing out to a deliriously joyful trio of nations from Scandinavia. Vanuatu's ranking caused some measure of consternation from other nations beaten by the tiny group of Y-shapes volcanic islands, especially those just below it like Australia and Canada. They argued that some of the 'happiness' criteria that had elevated Vanuatu to the top echelons had nothing do with the concept of happiness. The fact that Vanuatu didn't squander money on a military force, they claimed, should not be a factor in its happiness. Also, just because the nation was environmentally self-sufficient (mainly since most of the population was subsistence farmers), it did not necessarily mean it was happy.

The list's compilers countered these arguments by saying that countries without armies usually did not get involved in wars, and nations that were environmentally efficient usually had long living and happy populations. Mind you, perhaps the ranking should be taken with a pinch of salt. Take Bangladesh for example. This Asian country is not usually associated with high happiness and yet it comes out 26 places higher than the United Kingdom. Chad lies at the very bottom of the table, which is no real surprise as it's a nation beset by political violence and corruption, but the most surprising entry was for the nation in the second-from-last position. Who would have thought that Luxembourg would be such an unhappy little country?

We were in a traffic jam; mainly minibuses, the ubiquitous form of transport around the island. Instead of potholes, this time it was simply the number of vehicles. Fifty years ago, the road I was on was probably adequate. But without proper town planning, traffic had swamped the capital's transport network. But what was the solution? Knock down the buildings near the road so it could be widened? Build an expensive monorail system that sped over the traffic? No, Port Vila was doing nothing apart from trying to keep up with pothole repairs and placing a few policemen at busy intersections. So we moved forward, inch by monotonous inch.

The Grand Hotel and Casino was in the middle of Port Villa, just behind a large Bon Marche supermarket. The seven-storey hotel was one of the more expensive options in the town, but I was pleased I'd picked it due to its prime location. I grabbed my bags and headed inside another hotel in another Pacific nation.

3

The next morning was bright and sunny. I wandered down to the lobby as a door opened from the adjoining casino. Despite the relatively early hour, it was stuffed with people either sitting at slot machines or around card tables. A lot of them were women. When the door closed, I found a table in the hotel cafe and ordered a coffee.

Gambling among women was becoming a problem in Vanuatu. It said so in the local newspaper I was reading. It described how some women were spending much of their day playing cards and sometimes, shock horror, even boozing, to the point where their traditional mat weaving activities were grinding to a halt. Instead of picking up a needle and thread, the women were picking up a pack of cards and a bottle of Tusker.

Another news story said a school had been closed down because some of its pupils were possessed. I blinked at the term. I thought being possessed was only used in horror films, voodoo ceremonies or in Papua New Guinea. But apparently not, because a group of teenage girls had been behaving so irrationally that their teachers believed evil spirits had infected them. So, in the interest of everyone involved, the Headteacher sent the girls home. Better to have the parents sort them out than have the girls cause a fuss in the classroom.

I laughed at loud – what a ludicrous story. If teenage girls behaving irrationally were seen as extraordinary, then clearly Vanuatu did not have the same type of teenagers as the rest of the world. In the UK, every single school would be shut down.

Another headline warned of counterfeit notes circulating the capital. A woman working in a local shop had become suspicious of a 500-vatu note, worth about five US dollars, with which a man had paid for some goods. When she took it to the bank, they confirmed it was a fake, and so the newspaper wanted to educate the people of Port Vila on how to spot these forgeries. Again I laughed out loud, causing a man at another table to look my way. But I could not believe what I was reading: anyone but a simpleton would be able to see the difference between the real and fake banknotes because the fake ones had been printed at home on regular paper and then stuck back-to-back. They were hardly the work of a master counterfeiter.

The only other story of note was about the volcano over on Vanuatu's Ambae Island, but I knew about this because it had been on the news in Brisbane. The Manaro Voui volcano was one of the most active volcanoes in the world, continually breathing fire and smoke before having a rest for a while. Seven months previously, so much lava was frothing from its vents that the Vanuatu authorities ordered the complete evacuation of all 11,000 people who lived on Ambae Island. The locals had to leave everything behind, including their pets. A few months later, the volcano calmed down and the people were allowed back, dismayed to find their pets almost feral and on the brink of starvation. As the islanders considered this unfortunate turn of events, the monster awoke again, this time spewing so much ash that roofs collapsed and trees snapped. The situation, according to the newspaper, was ongoing, and the accompanying photograph showed people walking around with umbrellas; not to stop rain, but ash.

I finished my coffee and decided to investigate Port Vila.

4

I left the hotel and waded into the heat. From inside the air-conditioned interior of the hotel, the weather had looked inviting, but as the clamminess hit and the sweating started, the reality was less impressive.

Like Honiara's Kukum Highway, Port Vila's similarly spelt Kumul Highway ran through the length of the small town following the line of the ocean, which more often than not was obscured by buildings. I found one gap, though, and gazed at a luxurious view of Vila Bay, the most gorgeous slice of Pacific Ocean I had seen so far on my travels. The different shades of light blues and greens were astonishing and looked so inviting that I almost waded in there and then.

In the middle of the bay was a small island owned by the Iririki Island Resort, a brochure-perfect tropical idyll, once home to a British hospital but now catering for rich tourists. Accessible only by boat, the hotel owned a little ferry which transported guests between Port Vila and the island in just three minutes. After a few private moments of blissful staring, I walked to Port Vila's Central Market.

In many ways, it was similar to Honiara's Central Market, in that it was brimming with fruit and vegetables, but as well as bartering and selling going on, there was a bit of a commotion. As I was checking out some bananas to buy for breakfast, a woman at the far end of the market shrieked. A half a second later, another woman did the same thing and flung herself backwards. A few people were pointing and shouting. When some went to look at what was going on, I joined them.

The source of the commotion was no longer there, but judging from the snippets of conversation, a centipede had been in the women's midst. And it was a brute, according to the first woman who had seen it. She was spreading her arms out, indicating that the centipede was about two feet long. She gave the impression it had been about to eat her.

Vanuatu has no venomous snakes, venomous spiders or saltwater crocodiles, but it does have the some of the biggest centipedes in the world – beasts that bear no similarity to Europe's tiny pipsqueaks other than the number of legs. No, these are monsters from Hell, usually red or orange, with spindly legs that can propel the critters at staggeringly fast speeds. Growing to about 20cm long (well shorter than the women had suggested but still long enough to give pause for thought) to witness one on the move is terrifying. However, it is the curved, dagger-like pincers at the front that are its most disgustingly horrible feature. Anything with pincers is horrid, in my opinion, but the giant centipede takes things to a new level because its pincers are enormous and venomous. After it grabs its prey, it jabs them deep into the victim's flesh, injecting some terrible venom that can kill insects, lizards and small rodents in seconds. Then it devours them. A giant centipede is not fussy what it eats: anything shorter than its length is fair game.

From the hubbub of excitement and chatter going on, I gathered the stall holder who had first seen the centipede had been moving a box of mangoes. As soon as she'd caught sight of it, she had done the right thing by backing off. Though they try to avoid attacking people, if cornered they can become aggressive, and a bite from a giant centipede is no laughing matter. The wound will swell up and cause horrific pain or, in the case of an eight-year-old girl from the Philippines who was bitten on the head by one, even death. Hers remains the only death by a centipede in recorded history

Later that day, when I read about Vanuatu's centipedes, I came across a few more horror stories. One involved a man who had just picked up his gardening gloves. Unbeknown to him, inside one of the glove's fingers, lurked a giant centipede. As he thrust his hand in, it let rip, sinking its pincers into the soft flesh between two of his digits before making its swift multi-legged escape. All night the man writhed in agony, his painkillers having little effect on the horrendous pain rocketing up and down the length of his arm.

Another centipede horror story was about a man minding his own business when saw one of the orange demons racing towards him, legs going ten to the dozen. After dancing a scary jig to avoid its first charge, the man stamped on it but only succeeded in bringing one flip-flopped foot onto the end of the centipede. While he wondered what to do, the critter writhed, curled and then sank its pincers into his exposed foot. He ended up in hospital, shocked and broken.

Then there was the tale of a young man who went to bed one night. Sometime during the hours of darkness, his pillow dropped to the floor. In the time it took for the man to stoop and retrieve it, a giant centipede took up residence inside its folds. The man placed the pillow underneath his head and promptly fell back asleep. The next thing he knew was when two awful pincers jabbed at his closed eyelid. He tried to grab the orange assailant but it had already gone. Needless to say, after a painful recovery, the man spent many a night quivering under his mosquito net.

The commotion in the market finally died down and people returned to their stalls, including the two women who had seen the centipede. I left them to it and walked outside to eat the banana I managed to buy. But then, after walking up and down the street, I deemed it unremarkable and so stopped in the Jungle Café for a coffee, diligently checking my seat and general area for centipedes. That done, I sat and savoured the fact I was my third Pacific nation. Vanuatu was the most tourist-friendly, and cleanest, so far. It might also win the award for the most picturesque, but now that I had exhausted the main strip, I wondered what else I could do.

There were a couple of churches I could visit, plus a museum and a craft market, but they were hardly top-drawer tourist sites. With some free Wi-Fi, I looked at a map of Port Vila. The main core of the town, where I was now, was on one side of a thin peninsula. On the other side, near a lagoon, was the Holiday Inn hotel. Google Maps told me it would take thirty minutes to walk there. That was do-able, I felt. I could have a look around and maybe get a drink. That decided, I finished my coffee, paid the bill and set off.

5

At first, the walk wasn't too bad, but then I came to some steps. Google Maps had failed to show that massive hill that ran down the middle of the peninsula. The only way to reach the other side, apart from a ridiculously long coastal detour, was to climb the steps up the hill. With the ambient air temperature heading into the red, I started my ascent. At the halfway point, flanked by skittish lizards and fruit-bearing palms trees, I stopped for a breather and to wipe my furrowed brow. When my pulse calmed slightly, I carried on, willing my body upwards, forcing it to not give up despite the gradient. Then I saw a woman walking down towards me. Even though my heart was hammering and sweat was sluicing down my neck, I nodded and smiled as she passed; giving the impression I was out for a mid-morning stroll. She gave me a funny look in return but I did not care because I could see the summit. Once there, I bent double and held onto my quivering thighs. Then I downed my small bottle of water and tried not to collapse. Should a centipede attack now, I'd be fair game.

At the top of the hill was a dusty road called Winston Churchill Avenue. Across from it was an ugly set of low-level structures surrounded by spotlights, a tall fence and coils of barbed wire. It was Port Vila's men's prison. Built by the British during World War II, it housed around fifty men, packed together without air conditioning but plenty of bed bugs. The inmates were the usual cohort of thieves and robbers and six young Indonesians imprisoned for murder.

The men had been employed as fishermen, along with twenty other crew members, to work the waters of the South Pacific. After sixteen months of gruelling work, sometimes for up to twenty hours a day, the men grew weary, especially after being forced to eat fish bait to supplement their meagre diet. Another issue was that none of them had been paid since setting sail. The Chinese captain of the fishing boat was not helping matters; he didn't seem bothered about their concerns and seemed to take great delight in beating his crew if he found them shirking. So one night, the six Indonesian men, armed with gutting knives, scissors and hammers, stormed the captain's cabin and killed him. Afterwards, they stuffed his body into a fish cooling box and told the rest of the crew what they had done. When the vessel arrived in Fiji a few days later, the six were arrested and deported to Vanuatu (where the fishing boat was registered) and each was sentenced to 18 years in prison. When a newspaper interviewed the men, they seemed upbeat about their incarceration, saying that the conditions in Port Vila prison were far preferable to what they had endured on the fishing vessel.

I walked by the prison and then passed a few large homes of the rich. Each detached bungalow featured a sloping roof and an extensive veranda, reminding me of houses I had seen in rural Australia. What was nice to see was that each house stood in a garden devoid of security features, even with a prison in the vicinity. In Port Moresby, similarly placed homes would need armed guards and trip wires.

Further along, I came to Independence Park which, under normal circumstances was a cricket ground but, when I arrived, was a place of tents and tethered animals. I assumed it to be an agricultural show, especially with the tractors parked at one end but, as I walked through, I saw stalls selling arts and crafts, a stage with a reggae band and a tent selling toilets. Then I found a booth dedicated to something quite extraordinary. It was all to do with plastic.

6

Plastic pollution is an ever-present problem for many Pacific nations. A lot of this plastic comes from other countries not disposing of their trash correctly which then ends up washing onto their beaches, but a lot of the plastic is home grown. Vanuatu's situation has not yet reached the critical state of other nations, but the forward-thinking government was not going to wait for the problem to solve itself, and the tent I found myself in was full of information about their efforts at reducing plastic waste.

I read that a recent study found out almost seventy percent of litter found on Vanuatu's beaches was plastic or polystyrene packaging. So, in an almost unprecedented move, the government passed a law banning the sale of plastic bags, plastic straws and foam take-away boxes. They are the first country in the world to do so.

Presiding over the tent was a local woman wearing a T-shirt saying she was a member of the Vanuatu Environmental Science Society. She joined me at a display showcasing a naturally-woven bag that could be used instead of a regular plastic bag.

"Is it working?" I asked, pointing at the bag. "Are people using these?"

"Some are; I think it's a matter of time for the rest. The ban's not in place yet, so people have time left to use the plastic bags. But eventually, they'll have to use bags like this, or keep the same plastic ones they've got."

I told her about how clean Port Vila was in comparison to Honiara and Port Moresby.

"I'm glad you said that – those countries are a little behind us, but that's because they have other problems. Our problem is we need to educate our people. They're used to buying food from takeaways in polystyrene boxes and throwing the rubbish away on the street. We're telling them to have more pride in Vanuatu: to put their litter in a bin and to stop using plastic bags and straws. No one needs to use them anymore. The government helped our cause by banning them."

I left the stall buoyed by the forward-thinking actions of the Vanuatu government. They had taken a stance of which other countries ought to take note.

Back on the road to the other side of the peninsula, I came across a kava house. It offered, according to its colourful hand-painted signage, not just regular kava but the 'best qulitty' kava.

Kava is hugely popular in many of the Pacific nations, especially in Vanuatu and Fiji (where it is called grog). It is famous for its relaxing effects on the body. Historically, after a long hunt, tribal men would ease their aching muscles and weary tendons by imbibing kava. Alternatively, chiefs might offer it to esteemed guests to relax them. A few minutes after downing it, the kava drinker will feel stress-free and at one with the world. A side effect is that their tongue may go numb but this is sometimes a desirable outcome as unflavoured kava is an acquired taste: earthy, chalky and exactly like how most people would imagine a root to taste. However, unlike cannabis or alcohol, the kava drinker will not be cognitively impaired. All he or she feels is calmness and a sense of well being.

How it's made is as follows: first, the root of a kava plant is dug up, mashed and added to water to make a paste. This process takes a long time, but once it has been mixed and crushed sufficiently, the gloop is strained to separate the liquid from the pulp. This resulting drink is known as noble kava. Noble kava has been prepared like this for well over a thousand years and is still used today in traditional ceremonies (such as weddings and funerals) or as a way of winding down after a day's work. Rather like the local pub in England, the kava house offers a place for people to gather and enjoy a drink made the noble way.

However, making it the noble way is a bit laborious and so, an alternative, pre-prepared kava powder has been available in shops for years. Instead of a person doing all the hard work, a factory does it for them: Just add water and it is good to go. Along Port Vila's main street is a shop called the Kava Emporium, which describes itself as the 'Happiest Store in the World'.

In 2016, after much research, the World Health Organization declared kava as a low-risk to health unless the user drank it heavily or for long periods. If this was the case, then the drinker could expect a loss of appetite, red eyes, nausea and perhaps a feeling of general laziness – exactly how I feel every morning. Apart from that, they said, drinking kava was fine; possibly basing their conclusions on the fact that kava has been drunk in the Pacific islands for close to two millennia without any serious effects. This is why Australian immigration will allow a visitor to haul two kilograms of dried kava past customs without recourse. Likewise, the United Kingdom allows a person to have a stash of kava for personal use, even though they might be arrested if they try to sell it. Vanuatu regulates the quality of its noble kava, making sure that only the special stuff makes it abroad.

I might have gone to the kava house except it looked closed. But perhaps that was a good thing because in my current state of dehydration I'd have surely downed a litre of noble kava. God knows what would have happened then. As I traipsed away, I promised myself that I would try kava at some point on my trip around the South Pacific, but for now, I went in search of Captain Cook Avenue.

7

Because of its name, I envisaged Port Vila's Captain Cook Avenue to be the grandest thoroughfare in the capital, featuring statues of the great man and maybe a few life-size ships. I was wrong because it turned out to be a thin country road that offered access to a few small resort-type hotels, another kava bar, the city hospital and clumps of palm trees.

The only thing moving on the road was me, the traffic elsewhere for the duration of my walk northward. Occasionally a dog would bark from behind a wire fence or a chicken would appear to peck at the soil. Once I got past the buildings, the view was special, a muddle of lush green palms, papaya leaves and an ever-present blue sea. The water glistened like a mirage and it signalled a thought in my brain that I was thirsty, very thirsty. I needed water and I needed it now; so when I spied a sign that told me the Holiday Inn and Casino was only a short walk away, I quickened my pace.

The hotel was *nice*. It had everything a resort should have when located on a tropical island: a traditional-style lobby full of wooden carvings, a large swimming pool surrounded by palm trees, a golf course, a spa and, best of all, an area of prime beach bordered by a steamy body of water called the Erakor Lagoon. But I wasn't interested in any of that: only water. I made my way to the outdoor bar ordered a bottle of it. "No, make that two," I croaked at the bemused barman.

He went to the fridge, removed two bottles and then, inexplicably, placed the water near his till at the rear of the bar while my tongue thickened. As he fussed on something unseen under the counter, I looked around, wondering why the hotel was empty. I was the only person there and I wasn't even a guest of the hotel. The barman produced a couple of paper serviettes from under his counter and placed them carefully in front of me. Then he went back to his cash register. That was when I leapt at him, grappling him to the ground in my fury for water. Or at least that was what my mind did while I waited for him to ring the cost of the bottles into his damned till. And then they were mine and I greedily gulped.

"You thirsty?" the barman quipped.

I ignored him and downed an entire bottle. Then I fished about in my wallet for some vatu, the local currency, and handed it over. He nodded and went to the till again.

"Where are all the people?" I asked upon his return.

"Probably staying away because of the cyclone."

I did a double step. Maybe I was delirious. "Did you say cyclone?"

"Yep."

"What? And it's coming here?" I could feel a distant edge of panic.

"Maybe here or maybe Fiji. They're not sure. But it's not a cyclone yet, but they reckon it will be. It's not due for another week. Still, it's put a lot of tourists off I reckon."

I was still finding it hard to process the fact that a cyclone was whirling its way across the Pacific Ocean. And why was I only finding out about it now? The newspaper that morning had made no mention of it. And what made it worse was that I was meeting my wife in Fiji in a few days. She was flying over from Sydney. The last thing I wanted was for us to spend our time hunkered down in a hurricane shelter.

"What happens if it turns into a cyclone and hits Vanuatu?"

"We'll close the hotel and go to the shelters."

"What happens if it hits Fiji?"

"They'll do the same."

I nodded and morosely took my second bottle of water to the beach, plodding onto the sand and thinking about a cyclone and yet sufficiently coherent in thought to realise that the Holiday Inn's strip of sand was the first brochure-type beach of my South Pacific adventure.

Its windswept crescent of sand, nestling against the clear blue water of the lagoon, was overlooked by a forest of slender palm trees. Even better, was the total absence of tourists worried about the tropical storm rip-roaring in from somewhere in the distance. I took a few photos and then wandered into the lobby where I found some Wi-Fi.

Into Google, I searched news about the storm and found out the barman was correct: forecasters were warning of a tropical depression currently intensifying as it headed in the general direction of Vanuatu and Fiji. They reckoned it would almost certainly turn into a cyclone in the next 24 hours, and it would be a strong one. According to meteorologists, if it hit Vanuatu, it would make landfall in the next four or five days. If it hit Fiji, it would be a couple of days after that. In four days I would be on my way to Tonga and my wife would be on her way back to Sydney. We should be okay.

I left the hotel and thought about things. Even though I was probably going to be two or three days ahead of the cyclone, the potential for travel disruption could be enormous. I would keep my eye on the burgeoning tempest for the next few days. However, with no way to alter the course of Mother Nature, I decided to carry on with my sightseeing of Port Vila.

8

The Vanuatu National Museum lies opposite the Parliament of Vanuatu. It was the parliament I found myself drawn to first. Unlike most parliament buildings, Vanuatu's was largely unguarded. I could have walked up to the door unhindered had I chosen too. If I had not known it was the parliament building, I might have believed it to be a hotel, especially with the thatched roof and tropical greenery in its gardens. For a place of lawmaking, I could think of no better location in which to work.

The museum behind it was large but dimly lit. It was also stiflingly hot due to the lack of air conditioning and its motionless ceiling fans. A man was talking to a couple of Westerners at one end of the huge exhibits hall, pointing at something on the floor, perhaps a pot, and so I walked to the other end, looking at totems, statues and old paintings. Most of the figures were of large-headed men with impossibly huge eyes. One individual had a cloth-covered penis on show.

I studied a painting dating from 1880. It was jauntily entitled: *Cannibal Feast on the Island of Tanna*. When first exhibited in Victorian-era Liverpool, the painting caused shock and outrage, especially when the artist, Charles Frazer, claimed he had based his picture on what he'd witnessed himself.

The artwork was detailed and showed a group of naked men carrying a sturdy pole horizontally between them. Tied and dangling from the pole was a naked man. Another section of the painting showed a bound man on the ground. Standing above him was a cannibal armed with a sharpened stick. On the left-hand side of the grim picture, a figure adorned with a necklace of bones, stood over what looked like a fire. And in the background, scores of people waited for the feast to begin. Though Frazer's art did not show anything approaching gratuitousness, the implied horror was enough. It was so macabre that I stared at it for a long time in uneasy silence.

Another section of the museum offered information about a legendary chief with the improbable name of Roy. In the Thirteenth century, following a peaceful reign, Chief Roy died and, as was the custom at the time, he had a grand funeral involving copious kava drinking and plenty of dancing. When everyone was relaxed, some of the chief's closest friends, including his wife, were placed in the grave next to him so they could be buried alive. When there was enough topsoil covering them, a troupe of people literally danced on the grave to compact it further. Then everyone waited one hundred days for part two of the funeral experience.

Three months later, the second bout of kava drinking commenced, and this time more members of Roy's clan opted to be buried alive. In they went freely, but one woman did not go willingly. When a French archaeologist discovered the grim tomb of Chief Roy in 1967, he noticed that her skeleton had been bound with rope and therefore she was most likely buried under duress. He hypothesised that the position of her skull suggested she had been trying to raise herself out of the grave to breathe, but either fatigue or lack of air had stopped her from doing so. There was a photo in the display cabinet that showed two skeletons. One of them had its hands and feet tied with cord. Its head was slightly elevated. It was a ghastly photograph and I couldn't bear to linger on the notion of being buried alive and so left the museum.

9

The next afternoon, the weather was great with no indication that a storm was coming. In fact, it was a storm no longer, upgraded overnight to a fully-blown cyclone. It even had a name: Cyclone Keni.

I was inside a minibus on the way to visit a small island off the northeastern coast so I could do some snorkelling. One of the other passengers was a thirty-something Aussie called Dan. Due to the lack of seats, we were sitting together for the ride.

Dan told me he was a maths teacher in Sydney but had taken a year off to go travelling. Vanuatu was his first stop, and one of his main missions, apart from seeing the sights, was to play cricket.

"Cricket?" I said. "I thought it was rugby that was popular in the Pacific Islands?"

"It is but they also love their cricket. Before I flew here, I emailed a couple of cricket clubs and, when they found out I was an Aussie, they were well up for me playing a few games. I'm hoping to get a match tomorrow."

I asked Dan whether he was worried about the approaching cyclone.

"A little. But I reckon it'll miss Vanuatu. It's looking like Fiji will take the hit."

"That's where I'm heading tomorrow. I'm meeting my wife there. She's flying in from Sydney."

"Oh, mate. Let's hope it misses Fiji as well."

Forty minutes after leaving Port Vila, the minibus pulled up at Port Havannah, a grand name for a tiny coastal village. During World War II, American troops had established a seaplane harbour there but there was nothing left of that. Dan and I climbed out with our fellow island hoppers and headed towards the boat. Once aboard, I surveyed the ocean with the sharp eyes of a snorkeler. The water looked clear and delightfully blue, perfect for seeing fish and coral, and perhaps even turtles. Clear water would also make it easier to spot sharks.

Sharks, I was dismayed to learn, loved the warm water surrounding Vanuatu's many islands. Indeed, when I'd checked into my hotel in Port Vila, the man behind the desk had warned me against swimming in Vila Bay, the body of water between the hotel and the Iririki Island Resort because a tiger shark had been spotted there recently. A fishing boat ejecting bloodied fish remains into the harbour had attracted it.

Another shark story happened in 2005 when a family from New Zealand hired a boat to explore one of the islands. After mooring their yacht near a beach, the family decided to go for a swim, despite warnings given by a local man who told them it was not safe to do so. He pointed out a nearby fishing boat that was swishing water over its deck to clean it of fish guts and blood.

The family brushed his warning aside and jumped in, satisfied it was safe due to other local people already swimming there. Ten minutes later, a shark snatched their seven-year-old daughter. She reappeared seconds later, minus a leg. Despite her father getting her to shore, the blood loss was too great and she died.

"Are you worried about sharks?" I asked Dan as we set off in a glass-bottomed vessel. Our destination was Lelepa Island, renowned for its underwater life and unspoilt natural beauty. A foursome of Japanese tourists was seated across from us peering over the side of the boat into the shallow water. The other passengers were couples or families with children.

"Not really. I used to be when I surfed off Bondi. But since I stopped surfing, I don't think about them. Why? Are you?"

"No," I lied, scanning the depths for sharks. Then I pulled my gaze upwards and began to admire the view above sea level. It was a truly dazzling picture: pristine tropical water caressing a stunning white beach belonging to the mainland. Behind the beach, verdant hills flourished with thick vegetation. We were only minutes into our trip.

The man in the driver's seat of the boat picked up his microphone. "Guys, if you look to the left, you might notice some huts behind the palm trees."

Everyone looked.

"That's where the ninth season of *Survivor* was filmed."

Everyone looked even more.

Survivor was a US reality TV show, where a group of strangers is deposited in an isolated place for six weeks, to fend for themselves while cameras record their most exciting moves. Every now and again, the public will vote one person off the show so that, by the end of the run, one contestant can be crowned the winner and walk away with a million dollars.

"But do you want to know a secret they don't want you to hear," added the boat man enticingly. "When people watched that series on TV, they probably reckoned the contestants and crew stayed in camp, yeah? Well, let me tell you the truth: every night, they'd all pack their gear up and stay in a hotel. The crew, the contestants: everyone."

The Japanese contingent didn't know how to react to the information. I wasn't convinced they understood what the man had said, but maybe I was wrong because, after a short conference, all of them snapped a photo of the identified camp. I took his information with a pinch of salt. Although I had never seen a single episode of Survivor I thought it unlikely that the contestants would be whisked off to a plush hotel come nightfall. If they did, then surely that titbit would have come out in the media sometime during its 37 seasons.

Lelepa Island was a dense green mass encircled by shallow aquamarine and turquoise water. Now that we had stopped, the glass-bottomed boat, mostly useless on the voyage thus far, was offering a bountiful view of coral and tropical fish. Everyone on board peered through the glass, mesmerised by the spectacle as the captain dropped anchor. It was as if someone had placed three TV screens on the bottom of the boat playing footage from a tropical aquarium. Then the tranquillity of the moment was broken by the sound of an outboard engine. Some locals were speeding past us to set up stalls on the beach.

Dan waited for the Japanese group to jump into the water with their snorkels and GoPro gizmos and then dived in next. When he wasn't dragged under a cloud of red, I asked him about the water temperature.

"Like bath water, mate." He turned over so he could float with his facemask down in the water.

I waited for everyone else to go in then took the opportunity to speak to the boat driver. "Any sharks around here?"

He nodded. "Sometimes. But none right now." He turned back to his newspaper.

"How do you know?"

"Because I've checked. Besides, it's only at dusk that they come."

I sighed and returned to the back of the boat where the ladder was. The water was crystal clear and I could see shimmering stripy fish darting around the coral and sand. I climbed down the first rung and immediately regretted it.

With only my feet in the water, the freezing temperature invaded my knees, my thighs and my testicles. Bath water? Ha! Where had Dan last had a bath? In a Victorian workhouse in the depths of winter? The water was Arctic.

I decided to prolong my agony by submerging myself a step at a time until there were none left. Then, after a quick realisation I was actually going to do it, I flung myself in. After a few seconds of chest-tightening cold, my body adjusted and I put my face down into the sea. It was amazing: a palette of colourful coral, striking starfish, fluttering anemones and darting angelfish. I floated around, occasionally propelling myself with a swish of my arms.

When I came up to clear some water from my mask, the boat driver shouted in my direction. "Shark!"

I couldn't do anything. I went numb. And then the man laughed. It was the guffaw of a man who has told a good joke. "Sorry, I meant turtle. A green turtle. If you look here, where I'm pointing, you'll see."

I swam over and looked downwards. And by God, he was right. There it was: an adult turtle gently paddling its giant flippers towards a clump of sea grass. While I watched, it nibbled for a moment, and then swam deeper until it became a faint shadow. I ended up being the only person to see it.

Once ashore, we looked at necklaces, bowls, bracelets and things made from coconut shells. Dan walked straight past the beach stall, and I was tempted to do the same; in the end, I bought a thin fabric bracelet out of guilt.

"Have you seen the sand?" Dan asked. He was studying a handful. I stooped and collected some. From afar it had looked like regular sand, and yet, up close, I saw that each component was a miniature piece of intricately fashioned white coral, coiled, perforated or dotted with tiny holes. Each tiny sculpture had been smoothed and rounded by tidal action so that anyone walking barefoot would not cut their skin. It was quite amazing.

10

The next afternoon, enjoying a beer and a burger in the airport departure lounge, I thought about my next destination: Fiji – a nation possessing such an evocatively tropical name that to most people, especially in Europe, it epitomised the whole South Pacific region. Palm trees, mesmerising beaches and people in grass skirts singing about happy times offered a once-in-a-lifetime holiday destination, somewhere to dream about going one day. That day, for me, was today.

I was looking forward to getting to Fiji, not only because my wife would be there, but because of this notion of Pacific perfectness. The only thing worrying me was the cyclone. According to the latest reports, Keni was heading towards Vanuatu's northern islands but would most likely miss the populated islands. But then, five later, it would probably hit Fiji. Five days was just enough time for me to fly to Fiji, have a couple of days with my wife and then get out of dodge.

Top L-R: *One of Port Vila's many kava houses; A small, but beautiful, view of the Pacific Ocean in Port Vila*
Middle L-R: *The coral beach of Lelepa Island; A woman walks down a street in Port Vila; Tusker Beer (note the hermaphrodite wild boar)*
Bottom L-R: *The beach of Lelepa Island; The Kava Emporium in downtown Port Vila; Me standing alone in the Holiday Inn*

CHAPTER 4. NADI, FIJI

Interesting fact: Fiji used to be called the Cannibal Isles.

Of all the smaller Pacific nations I'd be visiting, Fiji was the wealthiest according to the latest GDP figures. Its wealth was almost double that of Samoa and Tonga, and three times that of Papua New Guinea. This influx of money was mainly down to two things: sugar and tourism. The former was milled, bagged and exported in vast quantities; the latter imported by planes, cruise ships and yachts. Because of this inflow of foreign cash, the lives of many in the archipelago have altered: instead of subsistence farming, they have their own businesses. Instead of roughly-built shacks, wealthy Fijians relax inside luxurious waterfront condominiums. For Fiji's rich, life on the islands is indeed paradise. But not everyone is rich in Fiji.

The distribution of wealth in Fiji is uneven. And this is a relatively new phenomenon. In times gone by, all land was owned collectively by the people who lived on it but presided over by a chief. He wasn't much more prosperous than his subjects, but he was more important. And this is how things were for centuries, and not just in Fiji. Then, over time, the tribal structures disappeared in Fiji as Western influence came to the islands. However, the notion of chiefs lingered. These ruling families left the fields and moved to the cities, claiming the best jobs and best accommodation. Over time, they amassed more money than anyone else and, when people finally realised what had happened under their noses, it was too late: the rich of Fiji were living the high life and did not want to give it up so Fijian society could equalise. This elite and wealthy class is a bone of contention in the country. But this is not the only problem in paradise: there is also the issue of race, which traces its origins to the actions of the British Empire.

Between 1879 and 1916, the British transported 61,000 Indian men and women to work in Fiji's sugarcane plantations. These were not slaves, but indentured workers offered the chance of employment for five years. After their toil was over, the labourers were given the choice of returning home to India or remaining in Fiji. Due to the cost of paying for their own passage across the sea, the vast majority chose to stay, marrying fellow Indians and renting small plots of land in which to cultivate crops and rear livestock. Soon these plots grew and merged and then became thriving plantations. Things were going so well that their friends and relatives in India started to make their way over to the islands.

Nowadays, Indian Fijians make up forty percent of Fiji's population. Many are teachers, engineers, accountants, medical personnel and politicians. This last occupation has caused the biggest problem. Before 2006, Indian Fijians in key government positions naturally looked after the best interests of their fellow Indian Fijian businessmen. The same was true of Ethnic Fijians. The result: a political toing and froing threatening to destabilise the whole government. Something had to give. In the end, the armed forces stepped in and, in December 2006, staged a coup (the fourth in twenty years). The head of the military, Commodore Frank Bainimarama, declared himself the new Prime Minister of Fiji.

Bainimarama sought to win the approval of the Fijian population, stating that if he had not taken over, Fiji would be facing a dangerous future of paganism and cannibalism. A little extreme, people thought: cannibalism was long gone and most people were either Christians or Hindus, not likely to renounce their faith because of some ministerial arguments. On the other hand, perhaps Bainimarama was right to have stepped in. After all, he had put an end to the burgeoning political crisis that had threatened the welfare of the country. Plus, he'd done it without loss of life. But the downside of all of this was could they, hand-on-heart, support a government that was, in effect, a military dictatorship?

While the people of Fiji pondered, Australia and New Zealand applied sanctions on Fiji. Neither was happy that a military government had stormed into parliament and kicked out the elected prime minister. Then the Commonwealth got involved and ejected Fiji from their membership. Fiji didn't care and carried on with what it did best: serving cocktails in its beach resorts and packing cargo ships with sugar. For tourists, the coup hardly registered and Bainimarama clung to power. Seven years on, elections were finally held for a new prime minister so that no one could accuse the country of being a dictatorship. Bainimarama won, got Fiji readmitted into the Commonwealth and soothed relations with Australia. He is still Prime Minister today.

2

Despite the political bubbling and a storm chasing me across the Pacific, from three thousand feet, Fiji looked nice. *Really* nice. It was all light blues and aquamarines, untouched sand and thick greenery: Fiji's unspoilt western fringes were stunning. Soon we were down in Nadi, inexplicably pronounced Nan-di, and I found myself one of only a handful of foreign visitors. Most of my fellow arrivals were locals, it appeared.

Fiji gets close to three-quarters of a million visitors annually, the highest number of any of the small Pacific nations. Vanuatu receives 100,000 visitors per year, double the amount Tonga gets. Unsurprisingly, the Solomon Islands comes last, welcoming just 20,000 visitors per annum. But Papua New Guinea, the bad boy of the Pacific island group gets more visitors than Vanuatu, Tonga and the Solomon Islands combined. This statistic surprised me until I realised that visitors were not necessarily tourists. A visitor in Fiji or Vanuatu *is* probably a tourist. A visitor in PNG could mean anything from a security consultant, a mining engineer to a journalist investigating raskol gangs.

I exited the terminal with a Fiji entry stamp newly minted on a blank page of my passport. I sniffed the warm sultry air and instead of the aroma of coconuts I sensed a hint of diesel fumes from the assembled buses and minivans. I jumped in a taxi and told the driver the name of the hotel.

The taxi driver, a forty-something Indian Fijian man nodded. "Nice hotel."

I smiled at him from my rear seat.

"Here on business?" he asked.

"No, I'm meeting my wife. She arrived yesterday. We're planning on doing a bit of sightseeing tomorrow."

"Sounds nice. I wish I could go someplace abroad and do some sightseeing. I've never left this island. Taxi drivers don't earn enough money to do things like that."

Inwardly, I grimaced. I hated situations like this. Here I was, a wealthy man, he supposed, taking an expensive airport taxi to an expensive hotel after having flown in from somewhere. But what could I do? Open my wallet and hand him some dollars? Offer commiserations that he would take with a pinch of salt? I did neither and changed the topic entirely.

"Was it in Fiji where drivers had to change from driving on the right to the left?"

"No, that was Samoa." We were now leaving the airport perimeter. A large billboard said: Bula! Fiji Welcomes You.

"When was this?"

"A while ago. Maybe about ten years now."

I asked why the Samoan government would do such a thing. After all, I could not think of another country who had decided to switch driving sides.

"The only cars they could use were expensive left-hand drive American diesels. Everyone else in the Pacific, like us, Australia and

New Zealand, were using cheap right-hand drive Japanese cars. So they went for that in the end."

Outside, the Fijian road system was pleasantly smooth and free of traffic. The land looked flat, apart from a distant range of brown hills. Everything seemed clean and well cared for. There was a MacDonald's, a JEEP company forecourt and something called Ken's Shopping Centre. Annoyingly though, the ocean I had seen when flying in had not yet revealed itself.

"What's the latest on the cyclone?" I asked the driver.

"They think it will hit Fiji. We still have four days. But that's another thing: if it does hit Nadi, and I can't work, will I get paid? I doubt it. It's already affecting my airport rides. I used to get ten, twelve fares a day; now I'm getting three or four. So that will be even less money this month for me." He shook his head and sighed.

We turned away from the heart of Nadi and headed north to Denarau Island, which on a map looked nothing like an island and instead just an extension of the coast. Built on a former mangrove swamp, Denarau was home to high-end hotels, a huge golf course and some mega-expensive residential dwellings. A road, known as the causeway, takes visitors there. Thirty minutes after leaving the airport, I was outside the Hilton, paying the driver and adding a tip to ease his woes. For the rest of the evening, I did nothing apart from fret over cyclones with my wife, Angela.

3

The next morning, Angela and I decided to investigate Denarau Island. We began the adventure by walking through an array of villas that made up most of the hotel's grounds so we could start at the ocean. "What did you say those gangs in Papua New Guinea were called?" asked my wife.

"Raskols."

"What a ridiculous name. That's what you call five-year-old boys."

I nodded in concurrence.

"I still don't know why you went there. Fiji, yes, Vanuatu yes; even the Solomon Islands, yes. But Papua New Guinea…"

"I know. But at least I've been now. And it wasn't that bad to be honest. I quite enjoyed it."

The beach area behind our hotel was as expected: a long arc of golden sand, drooping palm trees and a welcoming slice of bright blue ocean. It was a page from a high-end holiday brochure: faultless in almost every aspect. If someone were asked to conjure an image of a perfect tropical beach in their mind, this would be close to what they would see. But there was a problem: as dazzling as it was, I had seen the same beach in the Caribbean, in Indonesia, in Kenya and even in India. The only difference was this beach was deserted. Tourists were either keeping their heads down or hadn't arrived yet, not with Keni circling towards the islands.

"What do you think?" I asked my wife.

"It's gorgeous."

I nodded, looking up and down the length of the shore, lingering on a clump of coconut-laden palm trees hovering over the gentle surf. There was a hotel worker down there, straightening out some beach furniture. "But would you come all the way from Europe just to see this beach?"

Angela considered the question. "No. It's too far."

"Neither would I."

"It's absolutely beautiful; don't get me wrong. But it's just a beach. Coming from Sydney I can see the appeal of coming, but not from England, unless it was a stopover on the way to Hawaii or somewhere."

Instead of remaining to sunbathe, Angela and walked onward, passing the Sofitel, Weston, Sheraton and Radisson hotels, facsimiles of each other, all located along the same stretch of stunning beach. We were in paradise, but a slightly manufactured paradise, I felt.

We left the resorts and traversed a thin road that ran alongside the golf course. No one was playing when we passed. A couple of power joggers in Lycra were on the other side of the road: Western ladies of leisure. Further along, we saw a few residential homes overlooking a small inlet of the nearby harbour, homes that sold for around two million US dollars. The people who could afford them could also afford the sleek white boats moored next to private jetties.

"That boat has a strange name?" Angela said.

The boat was a large, white, double-decked yacht called *Elvis on Tour*. To be sure that we knew who the Elvis in question was, there was a painting of the superstar on the side: slick black hair and lips curled mid croon.

"Do you think he owned it?" I said.

"Who knows? But I doubt he would paint a picture of himself on the side if he did."

A short distance away was the Port Denarau Shopping Centre and Harbour, a tourist-friendly area of souvenirs shops, fruit stalls, tour booths, bars and restaurants, including a Hard Rock Café that had a giant guitar fixed to its exterior. The shopping centre was also home to a little shop devoted to hair braiding, one of the worst things anyone could do with their hair in my opinion. And the clientele is always the same: girls aged from six to twelve. Two girls, both sisters, came out of the establishment with their mother. The youngsters sported newly fashioned braids. Both looked ridiculous.

4

Angela and I decided to visit Nadi. Nadi was first developed by the British during World War II. They built an airstrip (now the international airport) and hid some artillery weaponry along the coast should the Japanese come knocking, which they never did. Back then, the Nadi Township, as they called it, was a backwater stop, swampy, hot and clammy; in constant danger of flooding. Nowadays, Nadi is a place to service the tourism and sugar cane industries, and is still prone to flooding, especially if a cyclone roars into town. The last time one came a few months previously, it washed homes away and transformed the main road into a river in which four people were killed.

The people of Fiji had done an excellent job at cleaning things up because if I hadn't known about the cyclone, I would never have guessed one had passed through. I wondered how the town would cope when the next one came in a few days.

Though not endowed with top class tourist sites, Nadi still offered a smattering of attractions so we hired a taxi and explained that we wanted to drive to all the major ones. The driver was agreeable to the proposal and signalled that we should climb into the back of his car.

Our first stop was the Sri Siva Subramaniya temple, located at the southern end of town, apparently the largest Hindu place of worship in the Southern Hemisphere. From the car park, it didn't look that big, but that was perhaps because scaffolding covered the central section. The entrance had a hand-painted sign which read: *strictly no smoking, no alcohol, no grog.*

Both Angela and I had to remove our shoes and also don colourful sarongs to gain entry, which a kind man in a small booth loaned us. A cane toad watched us with amphibious disinterest from some tall grass just past the entrance. Cane toads were introduced into Fiji's sugar cane fields to keep a lid on insect pests that could harm the crop. But they adapted to life in Fiji so well that they became pests themselves, especially with their toxic warty skin. We kept well away but soon realised why it was sitting on the grass and not the path. The path was hotter than hell and soon I was dancing a terrible salsa until I reached the sanctuary of vegetation.

"My soles are blistered off," I said, inspecting the underside of one foot, fully expecting to see flames and smoke. Instead, it looked normal; it wasn't even red. "Christ, that hurt. There should be warnings or something."

Angela was shaking her head at my patheticness. She was still standing on Beelzebub's pathway. Her feet were apparently made from lead. "Maybe not everyone's as weak as you."

"It's in my DNA."

"Oh, not that again."

A few months previously, Angela and I had sent some saliva samples to a company that offered DNA testing in exchange for cash. The results came back and told us about all sorts of useless but highly interesting bodily traits. For instance, my metabolism could handle copious amounts of coffee without any side effects. Angela's couldn't, which was ironic because Angela adored coffee. I could also detect the smell of asparagus in urine, which was something I thought everyone could do. My DNA also suggested I would have few freckles (true), green eyes (true), be bitten by mosquitoes more than other people (true) and have a full head of hair (I wish).

Then there was a serious little section of my report which offered information about diseases and conditions. It informed me I was unlikely to develop Parkinson's disease or something called Bloom Syndrome. But I was a carrier of cystic fibrosis. This meant if I had a child with someone who carried the same gene, there would be a 25% chance our offspring would have the life-threatening condition. Another snippet of information told me I had an increased risk of developing Alzheimer's disease, but I am hoping to forget this as I grow older.

Both Angela and I liked the little section that told us about waking-up times. If allowed to sleep unhindered by alarms or disturbances, I would most likely come awake at the quite precise time of 7.44 am. Angela's waking time was seventeen minutes earlier. But the one trait I took the most delight in reading referred to pain threshold. According to my DNA, I felt pain much more than the average person. Angela's DNA was simple and straightforward – no dodgy genes or unusual traits: she was as strong as an ox, whereas I was as weak as a kitten, as demonstrated by the pain I'd felt on my feet.

Luckily, a grass verge ran more or less parallel to the path and so I followed it, staring up at the decorations on the towering main section. Dedicated to the Hindi god of nature, I could see multi-armed deities sitting on ornate thrones set inside curved patterns of purple, blue, red and green. Specialist artisans, flown over from India for its grand opening in 1994, had handcrafted them. But the scaffolding was off-putting, like covering a painting with a net. After a quick walk through the other, smaller, shrines, where I developed a hitherto unknown talent at spotting shaded spots within hopping distance of my position, we decided to head into the town once and for all.

5

Downtown Nadi was no beauty. It would not even be described as attractive. At its best, Nadi was nondescript, especially the hodgepodge of unappealing buildings that flanked Queen's Road, the town's main and ugly thoroughfare. Untidy stores spilled out onto pavements, with names such as Cake World – The Cake Boss of Fiji, Rani's Variety Store and the quaintly spelled Kwality Store – House of Fabrics. Around the corner was Brother's Billiard & Grog Centre and a shop that offered hair braiding and massages. One of the biggest shops, rising ponderously through three yellow storeys, was Rups Big Bear, one of Fiji's home-grown chain department stores.

Angela and I crossed Queen's Road and entered Nadi Central Market. After seeing similar produce markets in Honiara and Port Vila, it was more of the same for me. But Angela wanted to linger and so we strolled past mounds of pineapples, mangoes, melons, bananas, coconuts and every other tropical fruit a person could think off. That done, we went back outside to visit a souvenir shop.

The shop we chose was large and devoid of other customers. When we entered, a thin middle-aged man looked us over with a practised eye. After correctly deducing we were not backpackers, he stood, smiled and introduced himself as Rishi, the proprietor of the souvenir emporium. "You are wise people," he told us. "You have picked the best souvenir shop in Nadi. All these artefacts are handmade and are one hundred percent genuine. Where are you from?"

I told him.

"Ah, England. You stopped the cannibals and gave us rugby."

Angela was looking at some dark-wooden masks that hung on a wall above a set of wooden penises with carved gecko's crawling up them. I was standing next to her, looking at some wooden bowls. None of the stock had prices on them which, to me, was a bad sign. Haggling was embarrassing, especially when we had no clue about good starting prices.

Rishi sidled in, deciding to focus his attention on Angela. "These masks are very special. They are called tiki masks – used to ward off evil spirits. If you have one of these in your home, you can be rest assured that your safety will be guaranteed."

I doubted that but asked him how much a mask cost. Not that we would buy it. I was surprised when the man answered my query straight away.

"Two hundred Fijian dollars."

I nodded thoughtfully as if considering the price. Two hundred dollars was about seventy pounds, way over the odds for a simple, though striking, brown mask. I then played my ace card. "It's a shame it won't fit in our luggage."

The man retorted quickly. "We can arrange shipping to anywhere in the world. We also accept Visa and MasterCard."

Damn.

But then, in an unprecedented move, Rishi changed the subject entirely. "Have either of you tried grog yet?"

I turned to him. "No. Not yet."

"Would you like to sample some? Free of charge, of course."

I knew his game. He wanted us to be under the influence of kava to make his sale. But I wanted to try it and when I turned to Angela, she was nodding, giving the go ahead.

We moved to a rear portion of the shop and sat on a carpeted area: me sitting alongside Angela, Rishi sitting in front. He had deftly crossed his legs and placed three items in front of him. One was a closed blue Tupperware box; another was a large wooden bowl containing an empty fabric bag; the third was a plastic bowl containing two polished coconut shells. Rishi opened the Tupperware box to reveal some grey powder that looked like cement. "This is the dried root of the kava plant. If you go to the market down the street, you can buy the actual root."

He produced a spoon from somewhere and shovelled in five hefty mounds of powder into the fabric bag. Then he added some water from a jug he had cunningly hidden behind him, squeezing and pressing the mixture until a grey soup began to seep into the wooden bowl. When he had a sufficient amount, he got one of the coconut shells, scooped in an amount and offered the bowl to me.

"You have to drink it in one go and then clap three times," Rishi instructed. By my side, Angela was smiling.

I took the bowl and regarded the grog. It looked like thin, grey-brown, cold tea. And then, without further ado, I downed the lot and clapped. It was horrible, like sucking on a root covered in clay.

"Good. Now it's your wife's turn."

Angela looked unconvinced and asked me what it tasted like. I felt I couldn't tell her the truth, and said it was okay. Angela downed hers and grimaced, forgetting to clap until Rishi reminded her.

By this point, my lips were starting to tingle and my tongue had gone numb. I felt quite good, to tell you the truth, and I quite fancied buying a large penis with a lizard climbing the shaft. We passed our bowls back to Rishi and he invited us to stand. I felt a little shaky as I did so but in fine fettle.

By the time we left the shop, we had bought a wooden bowl, a fridge magnet and a strange wooden implement that Rishi explained was a reproduction of a tribal fork. How everything would fit into Angela's luggage was anyone's guess, but she assured me it would. We walked along Queen's Road in high spirits. This grog was good stuff. Good stuff, indeed.

Back in our taxi, I inspected the fork again, which was quite unlike any fork I'd seen before. For a start, it was huge, about the length of my forearm, and instead of prongs, its end tapered into four lethal points that formed a circle. When Rishi had wrapped it, he explained it was a cannibal fork. Servants would skewer pieces of cooked human flesh onto the prongs and feed them to the chiefs.

Like many Pacific nations, cannibalism was once an integral part of Fijian tradition. Instead of killing and cooking people for the sheer fun of it, historical and archaeological evidence suggests the killings were only made after a battle as a symbolic way of vanquishing the enemy. When missionaries arrived on the islands in search of heathens, cannibal tribes saw them as enemies and so they often they went missing, presumed cooked. One missionary called Reverend Thomas Baker arrived on the Cannibal Isles in 1867, hell-bent on converting the islanders from their barbaric pagan ways. Together with seven Fijian converts, he set off into the hinterland but never returned. Following an extensive search, it was discovered that Baker and his group had been captured, cooked and consumed. Baker's shoes, charred and burnt, the only recoverable items found, now sit inside a museum in Sava, Fiji's capital.

It is no surprise, then, that in a nation once called the Cannibal Isles, the most prolific cannibal the world has ever seen once lived. Chief Udre Udre ate nine hundred people during his Nineteenth-century reign but, unlike most other cannibal leaders, Udre Udre didn't share the flesh. He ate every last piece himself and if he couldn't finish a meal, his underlings wrapped the meat in doggy bags for later consumption. It is reported that the only meat Chief Udre Udre ever ate was that from a human.

"I'd hate to be eaten by a cannibal," I said as I inspected the fork. "Imagine being cooked alive."

Angela nodded. "I think you'd be dead before they cooked you. But I do wonder what human flesh tastes like?"

"It's supposed to look like beef but taste like pork."

My wife considered this. "I bet it doesn't taste anything like pork." Suddenly she smiled. "If someone offered you a piece of human meat, cooked to perfection on a barbeque, maybe with some spices, would you try it?"

"No chance."

"What about for a million pounds?"

I was about to say no, then paused. A million pounds was a lot of money. I admitted that it would tempt me.

"What about half a million? And the person wasn't murdered or anything. They weren't diseased. They'd signed a piece of paper saying you could cook them. It's all legal and above board."

And so it went on. My lowest price point for sampling a bit of human was £500.

6

The next morning, Angela and I were back at Port Denarau Shopping Centre, bypassing the stores for the actual port. The passenger terminal was a busy hive of people, either queuing for tickets or wondering where to queue for tickets. The number of people surprised me: with a cyclone due in a few days, I thought the country would be empty of holidaymakers.

I scanned the check-in desks for the name of our tour company; scores of other tourists were doing the same thing. I looked at the head of one line, observing the long process taking place. Whenever a person approached the desk, forms had to be checked and printed. Discussion ensued as leaflets were handed over, and questions asked: delay, delay, delay. Eventually, we found the right line and discovered it so long that it curved off at ninety degrees around the ends of other lines. The situation was chaotic at best, and I was regretting booking the trip already. By the side, Angela told me to calm down. "This should have come up in your DNA test: Prone to queue rage: high."

Online, and peppered with evocative language, the tour had described a short voyage to somewhere called Beachcomber Island: the name alone sounding alluring in the extreme. 'Soak up the sun on the boat's deck,' the website claimed. 'Cruise past gorgeous islands as you make your way out into the clear waters of the Mamanuca Islands.' There was also the possibility of seeing dolphins and turtles. And, once at our destination, we could expect to see a 'picturesque marine sanctuary on a dream island.' That was it; we booked it there and then, rubbing out hands in glee and the prospect of such a voyage.

"This is not what I expected, though," added Angela, regarding the queue and mayhem. A Japanese couple in front, armed with floppy hats and snorkelling equipment, were muttering and gesturing at the queue. At the head of the line – about seventy people away – a middle-aged couple was getting a long-winded spiel from the woman working behind the desk. The check-in system was ridiculous and I was tempted to give up on the whole thing. Just then, a terminal worker walked along our line and shook his head. He looked at us all and stopped walking. "No queue here!" he barked. "You are blocking the other queues!"

He was right, but what else could we do?

"Everyone needs to move." He flapped his arms for effect.

No one moved.

He sighed louder and then scuttled off to find a gun. Or a cannibal fork.

Eventually, we had our tickets and then joined the scrum to board the vessel. I strained my neck to see the craft – a dull silver-coloured ship that hadn't even been painted. It looked like it had been delivered from the boat factory at the lowest price. A bare-bones boat would probably mean minimal service at low cost. Angela and I prepared ourselves for what promised to be an uncomfortable journey to Beachcomber Island.

7

The trip to Beachcomber Island wasn't as bad as we'd feared. Yes, the boat was packed, and yes, the seats were a little uncomfortable but as we traversed the tranquil waters between the Mamanuca Islands, the breeze soothed us and the view wooed us: a horizon of desert islands lying on top of a layer of iridescent blue.

Beachcomber Island was a small, teardrop-shaped, splodge of gorgeousness that appeared like a mirage, starting small but growing bigger and bigger until, in the last few minutes, it took up most of the view. I could imagine being an Eighteenth-century sailor, approaching the island with trepidation, wondering whether it would hold a bounty of coconuts and fresh water or a tribe of skull-bashing cannibals with bones dangling from their noses. Beachcomber Island epitomised the perfect South Pacific island getaway and, as soon as we pulled up on a slight sandbank, a group of singers plus a guitarist came down to the edge of the beach where they crooned a song rich with vibrant harmony and smiles.

Unlike Tom Hanks in *Castaway* (filmed on a nearby island) who found himself alone and depressed, we found ourselves walking across powdery sand en masse so we could gather inside a large building that sold beer, wine and burgers at ridiculously high prices. A buxom woman told us that we could now enjoy 'Bula Time', referring to the greeting that every tourist will hear in abundance during their stay in Fiji.

"You can snorkel," she told us. "You can wander around the island – it takes about ten minutes – or you can lie on the beach. But make sure you are back here by one o'clock for your lunch. Everyone okay with that?"

There were a few murmurs of accord, but not enough for the woman's satisfaction. "I said: is everyone okay with that?"

More agreement and nods.

The woman raised things a notch with a Club 18-30-style move. She yelled, "Say 'yeah' if you're having a good time in Fiji!"

Most people said yeah, but not exactly at full, all-excited, volume.

"No people! Come on: say 'YEAH' if you're having a good time in Fiji!"

More people said that they were indeed having a good time in Fiji, even though, at this particular moment, they probably weren't."

"I said: say 'YEAAAAH' if you're having a good time in Fiji." She raised her fist into the air to punctuate the word.

The room exploded into a chorus of zealous 'yeahs'. It was like we were in the hands of a mad evangelist. Sitting beside me, Angela rolled her eyes.

The woman then told us that if we wanted to go snorkelling, a boat was ready to take us straightaway. Almost everyone headed outside but, because the first boat filled quickly, a second was commandeered, which Angela and I found ourselves as the only passengers.

This was more like it, I felt: a private boat tour was just what the doctor ordered. Ten minutes later, still within sight of the island, we dropped anchor and looked down. Without a doubt, the water was the cleanest, clearest and most fish-filled I had ever encountered, even better than in Vanuatu.

"Any sharks?" I asked the man in charge of the controls, ever worried about being part of the ocean food chain.

"No sharks. Only sea snakes. But they will not attack unless you upset them."

And so we both went in, with me finding the water's temperature far more agreeable than the water in Vanuatu. And for the next thirty minutes, I enjoyed my own private aquarium filled with blue and purple parrot fish, stripy zebrafish, shimmering and darting blue fish as tiny as my little finger. Sometimes I'd spy a sea cucumber or a bright blue starfish, all of them living around the chaos of colourful coral.

Every now and again, I would catch a glimpse of Angela, but mostly I was a solo traveller gliding over an underwater world of absolute, unadulterated beauty. In short, it was spectacular, especially when I hauled myself up into the boat with having sighted neither serpent nor shark. Beachcomber Island was turning out to be great, and it made me wonder whether any actual beachcombers had walked upon its fine powdery sand.

8

Historically, beachcombers were Europeans eking out livings on Pacific islands by scouring beaches for anything of value with which to sell or trade. In an age of frequent shipping disasters, worthy pickings were usually easy to find, especially for knowledgeable men like beachcombers who were usually unemployed sailors. After finishing work on one ship, men would be dropped off at an island to amuse themselves while they waited for a new boat to take them up. But beachcombers were not always seamen between jobs; sometimes they were deserters sick of life on the high seas. By the 1850s, two thousand beachcombers were in operation around the Pacific.

On famous beachcomber was an American sailor called David Whippy. After his ship moored in Fiji in 1824, he decided to make a run for it, hiding until it departed without him. Then he started beachcombing and casting his eye over the local ladies. After learning a few words of their local language, he began courting them, eventually marrying four different women and having a large brood of children between them. Soon he was integrated into the local Fijian community, becoming a trusted advisor to a cannibal king.

Whether he personally partook in the 'long pig' feasts is unknown, but he would almost certainly have been present when others were munching on thigh bones. However, he never lost touch with reality because whenever a shipwrecked crew washed up on the island, he would help them out, acting as an interpreter to save them from the cooking pot. Mr Whippy eventually died in Fiji aged 70, reportedly happy with his end, leaving behind a brood of children and grandchildren. Many of his descendants still reside in Fiji, some of them in such proximity that the area is called Whippy Land.

Another infamous beachcomber went by the name of Charlie Savage. Unlike David Whippy's calming demeanour, Savage led a life full of violence. Supposedly a Swede, descriptions of the man are vague, with the occasional mention of a purple beard. After being shipwrecked off the coast of Fiji in 1808, Savage found himself alone and adrift. But since he already knew the local language (he had learned it while living in Tonga) Savage found he could communicate with the local cannibal chief. They made a deal: in return for not cooking him, Savage would show the chief special things he had never seen before.

Being canny, Savage knew that plenty of debris from sunken ships would be making its way ashore and, sure enough, when he combed the beach and found some muskets, he waited for them to dry before demonstrating their use to the chief.

The chief and his cannibal henchmen loved the weapons and so turned off the heat on the cooking pot and welcomed Savage into their tribe. He quickly found his niche, even marrying one of the local women as he enjoyed the odd slice of long pig. When other beachcombers arrived, Savage usually offered them two choices: be cooked with yams, or join his little fighting force. Most chose the latter and Savage's gang soon became a crucial part of the chief's battle group.

Savage was so effective with a musket and so violent in his killing of enemies that he was feared as being too ferocious even by cannibal standards. This is when you know you've gone too far. But no one told him to curb his bloodlust, especially when his tribe established itself as most powerful in Fiji. Instead, the chief bestowed a great honour on the man, allowing him to become a cannibal chief in his own right.

Alas, it did not end well for Savage; he was eventually killed during a battle on a neighbouring island and possibly cooked and eaten – a fitting way to go.

9

Back on Beachcomber's, bypassing the sunbathers and people paddling at the water's edge, Angela and I decided to traverse the whole island. It took longer than the ten minutes suggested by the woman at the start, but that was because we stopped to study starfish, crabs and the occasional seabird. It was almost like being a child at the seaside for the first time, picking through rock pools and staring into marine microhabitats.

"This is the life," I said, using the most overused phrase by people on holiday. We were standing near a pool filled with blue starfish as big as my hand. They looked like plastic toys.

"Was Vanuatu as good as this?" Angela asked.

"Not the beaches I saw. This one's amazing."

And it was, but, unlike the beaches near the hotel on Denarau Island, this one was real and not manufactured in any way. But we had to leave the starfish behind to complete our navigation of the outer edge of Beachcomber Island. After passing a forest of palms, we found ourselves back at the bar area and beach. After buying a couple of expensive Fiji Bitters, we retired to a table in the shade. Someone had left a newspaper there.

It was called the Fiji Sun and, as well as a headline about Cyclone Keni (which said that Fiji had issued some flood alerts), it featured a juicy double page spread called *Wanted People*. The police of Fiji were asking for the public's help in locating the whereabouts of a whole raft of people including someone called Sanjay who was wanted for theft. The accompanying mugshot showed a thickset gent with no neck and a no-nonsense smile. Another man called Talei was wanted for 'indecently annoying a person'. I pointed him out to Angela and she shook her head. "What does that mean?"

"I'm not sure."

Later we discovered that 'indecently annoying' someone meant the perpetrator had either threatened to send explicit text messages or had flashed his private parts.

Another member of the wanted list was Jeremai, a smiling grey-haired gent, sought after for 'general dishonesty' whereas Ashrita, one of the few women to make the hit parade, was wanted by the police for 'obtaining a financial advantage by deception.'

The only other story of interest led with the enticing headline: Law Student Charged with Witchcraft. The Pacific, it seemed, could not move on from its belief in sorcerers.

"Why can't England have headlines like this?" I said.

"Because we live in the Twenty-first century."

"So does Fiji."

The student in question, a somewhat mature 51-year-old man, had allegedly cast a spell on a woman that lasted three days. During this time he obtained hundreds of dollars from her bank account and then used undisclosed sorcery skills to fondle one of her breasts. Why he didn't fondle the other the article did not explain. Despite his powers, he was arrested; not because of his strange antics but because witchcraft was illegal in Fiji.

After completing another circumference of the island, this time in the opposite direction, we snorkelled and then did nothing for an hour. It was good to rest after such a great day.

10

The next morning, both of us were packing in preparation for leaving Fiji. Angela was flying back to Sydney, where I would meet her in a week. Looking at the sky through the window, it was hard to believe that a cyclone was going to hit Fiji in the next few days. The sun was a perfect blue. However, in preparation, all schools were going to be closed, starting the next day.

"So Tonga next," said Angela with some amusement. My wife could not understand my compulsion with visiting new countries whenever the chance arose. Sometimes neither could I, especially when the country in question was as remote as Tonga. "What will you do there?"

I shrugged. It was a good question and one I had no real answer to. I knew next to nothing about Tonga except that it produced successful rugby players. But I didn't have any idea what I would do when I arrived there. I told my wife I would play it by ear.

"I'll see you in Sydney in a week or so, then."

"That's the plan."

After a fond farewell, I left for the airport to catch my afternoon flight to the Kingdom of Tonga, leaving Angela to enjoy the hospitality of the Hilton hotel for another couple of hours. The fifth country of my Pacific nation odyssey was just a quick ninety-minute flight away.

Top L-R: *Angela and me enjoying Beachcombers Island; The Hilton Hotel offers some spectacular views of Fiji*
Middle L-R: *Tropical fish at the side of our boat near Beachcombers Island; Entrance to the Sri Siva Subramaniya Temple, under renovation; Fiji Bitters Beer – cooling on hot tropical days*
Bottom L-R: *Downtown Nadi is nothing special, apart for vendors offering kava-tasting sessions; Another beautiful sunset over the Pacific*

CHAPTER 5. NUKU'ALOFA, TONGA

Interesting fact: Apparently, Tongan women make good jugglers.

Tonga has a population of around 107,000 people, which is less than the number of people who live in the Isle of Wight. Most of them live on just one of the 170 or so islands that form the Polynesian kingdom. That island's name is Tongatapu, a bone-shaped block of land only 100 square miles in area, about the same size as the UK city of Birmingham. Formed from coral, the island of Tongatapu is mostly flat but covered in a thick layer of volcanic ash and soil which makes the land highly fertile. Instead of lovely beaches, the island's coastline is mainly rugged cliff faces lashed by strong ocean currents.

The first European to clap eyes on the island was a Dutch explorer called Abel Tasman. In 1643, he possessed a substantial quiff of black hair that complimented his thick moustache. When Tasman spied the island through his telescope, he saw locals wearing grass skirts and little else. Tasman didn't linger and moved onto the Americas.

Captain Cook came next and found the islands much to his liking, so much so that he named them the Friendly Isles. Unlike Tasman, he made landfall and, in return for a Tongan feast, Cook gave the local king a few pigs and a juvenile giant tortoise that he had picked up in Madagascar. The royal family loved the tortoise and allowed it to roam freely around the royal gardens for the next 188 years until its death. It was the oldest tortoise ever to have existed.

Things were not so friendly for another group of Englishmen who arrived in Tonga in 1806. When their ship dropped anchor, the captain invited a few local chiefs on board. After a quick meeting, the Tongans agreed to see the ship and brought a home-cooked feast with them. Some crewmembers were suspicious about this act of kindness, especially when they saw some of the Tongan delegation snooping around the ship, and told the captain of their doubts. He brushed aside their concerns, even threatening to flog some of them for sullying the motivation of their esteemed guests.

But the captain should have listened because the next day, a few hundred Tongans boarded the ship armed with clubs and spears under the guise of wanting to look around. When the captain was asked to go ashore to meet some village elders, his crew were dismayed when he agreed. As the captain stepped onto the shore, a large man appeared from behind a palm tree and clubbed him to death. At the same time, the Tongans aboard the ship attacked the crew, killing almost all of them. After clearing the ship of anything useful, the tribe set fire to it. It sank shortly afterwards.

One of the few Englishmen to survive was a fifteen-year-old ship's clerk called William Mariner. For some reason the local chief took a liking to him and so Mariner lived among the tribe, dressing in the same style and becoming fluent in their language. Eventually, he was rescued and arrived back in England as the world's topmost expert on Tonga, so knowledgeable that he was able to write a book about his experiences in the South Pacific.

2

From aboard the Fiji Airways turboprop, the island of Tongatapu looked bleak and windswept, its western cliffs pounded by choppy and swirling waves and chafed by low-level cloud. Instead of being a tropical beach island, Tonga looked like somewhere Emile Bronte might have written about.

As we flew over the coast, settlements appeared but were sparse. Each village was scattered around a thin road intersection with a church at its centre.

The capital city, Nuku'alofa, a word so hard on the eyes that it almost hurt, loomed to my left. Home to just 25,000 people, the capital of Tonga looked grey and portentous as it slid in and out of view between sheets of cloud.

And then we landed on the runway and were soon trundling to a small terminal building. As the aircraft doors opened and some little steps were produced, I noticed a small armada of golf buggy-type vehicles. Even though the terminal was an easy walk away, I was directed to take a seat in one of the electric cars and, when it was at its full capacity of six people, we drove for twenty seconds.

As the only arriving flight, transiting customs was simple: a smile, a stamp and a wave through into my fifth South Pacific nation.

Greeting me on the other side was a man holding a piece of paper with my name written on it. He was standing next to a trio of orange-shirted gentlemen singing and playing acoustic guitars. Whenever a passenger emerged from the terminal, they would rouse themselves into song.

The man with my name was Salesi, my taxi driver for the journey to the hotel. I was hoping the ride was going to be swift because it was already 3.30 pm and I had a lot to do.

The next day was Sunday, and Sundays in Tonga meant every shop would be closed. I needed to get to the hotel quickly so I could find a shop to stock up on supplies.

As well as all the shops being closed, Tongan Sundays were devoted to the church. No music played (except in church) and the people of Tonga were banned from doing chores on this holiest of days. If a household needed to wash and dry their clothes, they had to do it midweek or on a Saturday. Even doing a press-up could bring about a reprimand if attempted on a Sunday, as anything considered an 'activity' (shopping, swimming and exercising for example) was illegal.

A famous saying in Tonga stated that the locals only did three things on a Sunday: go to church, eat and then go to sleep.

3

"Will anything be open tomorrow?" I asked Salesi. The road from the airport was a simple two-lane strip of tarmac bordered by brown dust. Beyond the dusty verge was vegetation, with bushy trees and spindly palms sprouting from tall grass. In the time since landing, the sun had come out, casting away the cloud, engulfing the island in tropical heat.

"Nothing will be open. Well, the hotel will be, but only for an evening meal. If you're thinking of doing anything in town, then forget it. You'll have to wait until Monday."

I told him that on Monday I'd be flying to Auckland, to which I received a look of utter disbelief. I knew what he was thinking: why has this nutcase flown all the way to Tonga to stay for 48 hours, especially with half that time being on a Sunday.

We remained silent for a while. Outside the vegetation had thinned. Sporadic homes peppered the side of the road, all small but decent-looking one-storey structures. Dogs frolicked or lounged on the grass and dirt outside them.

"Who owns these dogs?" I asked.

"Most of them are wild. They scrounge what they can. At night, they sometimes form packs, so people around here get used to carrying a rock or two to scare them away."

This brought a distant memory of something I'd read. "Do people eat dogs in Tonga?"

Salesi smirked. "No one I know eats dog, but people used to a while back. But it was never a common thing or anything. It was poor people; desperate, you know. If someone is starving and the only meat is the pet dog, then that's what they're gonna eat, right?"

I nodded uncertainly. I could never imagine a situation where I would want to kill, cook and eat my pet dog. But then again, I had never been starving to death. To take my mind off eating dogs, I asked what tourists did on a Sunday in Tonga.

"As I said, everything will be closed, but you can walk around and see the palace if you want. Maybe go to the Royal Tombs. But there is one place you can go – a small island across the bay. A lot of tourists go there on a Sunday. If you get to the harbour, you can catch a boat to the island. It's called Pangaimotu. You can swim, lie on the sand and do a bit of snorkelling. There's a bar there that will be open so you can grab a beer and get some lunch. Ask your hotel; they'll give you the details."

That sounded okay, I felt. Visiting an island might be an option if Sunday did indeed turn out to be a washout. But for now, I sat back, waiting for Nuku'alofa to make its presence known. When it did, twenty minutes later, I saw that it wasn't much different from the villages I had passed. There were a few commercial buildings such as car dealerships, Chinese restaurants and small grocery stores, but that was about it. In the distance, I could see a tall building that looked like a church and something else that seemed important, but nothing to suggest I was in a capital city. Plus, the traffic was almost non-existent, which, in a way, was good because there are no traffic lights in Tonga. We skirted the town centre and hit a coastal road, the location of my hotel.

4

The hotel was a slice of white niceness spreading over three storeys; it had a little Italian restaurant on the lower level. Almost colonial looking, I was pleased with my choice of stay, especially since the hotel overlooked the Pacific Ocean. While I waited for a couple to check-in, I investigated my immediate surroundings. Instead of a sandy beach, the shoreline was muddy brown silt with large rocks scattered upon it. As uninviting to sunbathers as it was, a foursome of animals loved it: a mother pig and her brood of playful piglets. Mother pig, snout to the silt, was unearthing rocks in search of juicy things to eat. The lower portion of her body was covered in wet mud as if she was no stranger to wallowing in the shallows. Then she found something, something with a shell, judging by the sound of her crunching. The three piglets were on a drier patch of mud, close to mum, playing like puppies. It was a joy to watch.

Feral pigs are common in Tonga. According to a recent study, there are two pigs for every person in Tonga. They roam the streets of the capital, they laze about in people's gardens and sometimes the hogs try to force their way into shops to grab packets of crisps, but most of all they like to hang around on beaches waiting for the tide to go out so they can begin their snuffling. In Mu'a, a village near the airport, hundreds of these porkers enjoy nothing more than a trot in the sandbanks to find their next meal. But what is strange about Tongan fishing pigs is that they were never a natural species of the country. It was Captain Cook who brought them in the 1770s. Every single Tongan hog is a descendant of these original European imports.

I watched as another pig trotted from the side of the hotel and crossed the road towards the ocean with its stubby little legs going hell bent for leather. After sniffing a rubbish bin for a moment it headed out to sea, submerging its head into the water. It came up triumphant for it was chewing away on some salty sea morsel. It reminded me; I had to buy my own snacks before all the shops closed.

5

After checking into the hotel, I grabbed my shades and found myself walking behind the hotel in search of a shop. The track that led around the back looked almost rural, especially with pigs waddling around in the grass. There were dogs, too, both species of mammal seemingly happy in each other's company. One dog trotted up to me, its tail wagging high in the air. I'd once read that if a dog has its tail up, then it is a happy dog, and so this proved because the hound was almost smiling up at me, its tail swinging like a rotor. I ruffled its head and moved on, passing small homes with washing hung from lines and vacant prams or wheelbarrows sitting in their gardens. I could smell smoke from small fires burning at the bottom of some yards, but I could not see a single person except a man passing in a silver Toyota hatchback. He glanced my way and then was gone around a corner.

Some of the homes had suffered extensive damage. A two-storey house had most of the wood panelling from its upper level missing. Another had a damaged shed and a fence that had been knocked almost horizontal. A third home had a large section of corrugated metal roofing piled into a crumpled heap at the edge of the road. A few trees had been uprooted and shoved out of the way.

The damage was caused by a terrible cyclone that struck Tonga two months before my arrival, the same one that had ripped through Fiji. Cyclone Gita attacked Tongatapu with winds roaring up to 230km/h. Palm trees were torn from their roots, telephone poles snapped out of the earth like twigs and hundreds of homes were damaged or destroyed. Even the century-old Tongan Parliament House did not escape the onslaught: flattened to bits in just a few minutes. Two people lost their lives: one a woman who had remained in her house during the storm instead of seeking refuge in one of the hurricane shelters and another who had died of a heart attack during the worst of the storm. It was the worst hurricane to hit Tonga in six decades. So it was no surprise to still see the remains of Gita's damage.

After a good fifteen minutes of seeing nothing apart from houses, pigs and dogs, I turned back to the thin road that led along the coast. A sign told me where I should run should a tsunami come – in the opposite direction to the wave, preferably up a hill. Out in the ocean, some distance away and yet only in the water up to their ankles, were a dozen or so people carrying plastic bags, the first citizens I'd seen since the man in the Toyota. All were peering intently into the water or else swishing about attempting to catch fish and other sea creatures. One man, off by himself, seemed the most organised for he had a net, which he had cast wide in the shallows. This explained why he had the biggest bag slung over his shoulder. Another thing I noticed was that most of the people out in the sea were overweight. And they were not alone. In a 2018 study, Tonga was found to be the second-most obese nation on the planet, losing out only to fellow Pacific Island, Nauru. And one of the reasons Tonga is so obese is because of something called mutton flaps.

6

Mutton flaps are breasts of lamb, a cheap and cheerful cut of meat with a fifty percent fat content. They are hugely popular across the South Pacific, but especially in Tonga where locals will catch a healthy fish and then sell it so they can buy some mutton flaps.

The cheap cuts are imported from New Zealand where the meat is deemed unsuitable for local consumption. But to the people of Tonga, who see Western values and Western goods as an aspiration, mutton flaps are regarded as a refined delicacy. And it's not just shanks of cheap mutton that are on the menu in Tonga; the locals also have a penchant for turkey tails, another cheap offcut that the rest of the world eschews. A whole generation of Tongans has grown up with these cut-rate and nasty foodstuffs.

Six in every ten adults is obese in Tonga (double that of the United Kingdom), and most of those who aren't, are heading that way. In fact, on the flight over from Fiji, I had observed the cabin crew handing out oversized seatbelts in virtually every other row of the plane. But as well as the obesity epidemic, Tonga is facing a type-2 diabetes epidemic, with four out of ten people suffering from the condition. When King Tupou IV died in 2006, he had the dubious honour of being the fattest king to have ever lived, tipping the scales at a whopping 200 kilograms. And because of his size and position of power, he was regarded as someone to emulate. In Tonga, big is beautiful, where an obese woman is seen as more attractive than a slim one. But it's not just mutton flaps and turkey tails that are causing Tonga's widespread obesity; cheap canned meat such as Spam and corned beef add to the problem, together with the country's tradition of feasting at every opportunity. Banning exercise on a Sunday doesn't help either.

The government of Tonga is worried. And so they should be. With soaring diabetes, hospital bills are going through the roof. And unlike the majority of the world where life expectancy has been slowly increasing, in Tonga, it is dropping. Six years ago, the average Tongan could expect to live until 72; now it is 67. In a country where the average family has abandoned its meals of fish, vegetables and rice to embrace fatty meat, the government has its work cut out. As it stands, they are taxing the bad food, educating their children and persuading everyone to be more active (but not on a Sunday, God forbid). But nothing seems to be working, and the average Tongan continues to tuck into fatty cuts of lamb or imported cans of Australian Spam and appears unwilling to stop.

7

I carried on walking past the people in the ocean until I came to a corner of the road. A tall black fence interspersed with sturdy white columns blocked me from stepping forward. Instead, the road veered inland at right angles. But I stopped at the fence and peered through the railings, seeing an area of manicured green that belonged to the Tongan Royal Palace. At over a hundred years old and made mainly from wood, it was a miracle it was still standing after the cyclone. It was clearly well built because it looked in immaculate condition.

The palace was huge and stately, featuring a white exterior and burgundy roof, with towers, fancy columns, shady verandas and wide balconies. It reminded me of some exceptionally well-kept houses I'd seen in the Australian countryside, only on a much grander scale. I stared long enough to see if any people were about, perhaps the king himself, Tupou VI, a man who featured on the nation's banknotes, but saw no one except two members of the Royal Tongan Guard. They were standing a little to my right, guarding the entrance to the palace. Neither man had noticed me, so I walked around the edge of the fence to see if I could get permission to pop into the palace grounds to take a quick photograph.

One of the guards was older and rotund, and seemed to be in charge; the other was much slimmer, suggesting he had either not discovered the delights of mutton flaps or did not like them. Neither man was carrying a weapon that I could see. At the open gateway, the guards eyeballed me. I pointed to my camera. "Can I come in and look around?"

The older man shook his head. "No."

"Just to take a quick photo?"

The same man thought about this for a second or two as he looked me up and down. The younger man watched from his standing position near a flower bed. Finally, the boss spoke. "You can come in a little bit, and take some photos. But you can't walk around."

I thanked him, entered the gate and walked forwards, wondering how far I'd be allowed to proceed.

"Stop there."

Not very far, then. Nevertheless, I took a few photos, thanked the guards and left the palace grounds to carry on with my little walk, heading into the centre of Nuku'alofa.

Because it was Saturday evening, a time for fun and frivolity in most places, I was expecting to find the city full of shops, bars, restaurants and places of fervent business. Well, Nuku'alofa was nothing like that at all. In fact, it was like no other capital city I'd visited. Tonga was asleep.

Nothing was open except for a small café called Friends: Where Tonga Meets. It was housed inside a quaint wooden white building that stood on the corner of the main street. Inside, I spied a few Westerners having something to eat, but I walked into the adjoining gift shop. I was the only person there and so I walked back outside again, passing Canton Fast Food, Tuo Hai Hair Salon and the iCoffee Sport Bar. All three were closed.

I looked at my watch. It was past five pm, which meant that if I wanted to find a shop that sold provisions, then I'd better get a move on. I briskly turned a corner and saw a strip of shops that were all open, but none sold food – each specialised in household goods such as mops, kettles and wheelie bins. In desperation, I approached one shop with an open doorway. A Chinese woman sat at a small table just beyond the entrance. "Is there a supermarket around here?"

"Supermarket? No. Only shop."

"Okay, thanks. But where are shops I can buy food from?"

"All over." She looked back down, dismissing me as an annoyance she could do without. Frustrated, I left her store and carried on along the street and then doubled back when I found nothing that sold food. And then, about to give up empty-handed, I found my goal: a convenience store that was still open. It was small and it was dingy, but it sold crisps, biscuits, drinks and toothpaste, though none were brands I'd ever heard of except for the red tubes of Colgate. I grabbed two packets of biscuits, a couple of chocolate bars and three bottles of water. I looked for some beer but couldn't find any, but I did see some notorious mutton flaps in a freezer at the back. The fatty horrors, wrapped in plastic, were labelled as lamb flaps. They were the cheapest cuts of meat in the freezer. I considered buying them for research reasons but, when the man at the counter told me to hurry up because he wanted to close his shop, I left them for someone else to buy. As soon as I'd made my purchases, the man stood up and ushered me out. Then he pulled down the shutters to lock up. The last shop in Tonga had just closed its doors.

8

With my purchases, I wandered towards the huge and imposing Free Church of Tonga, the same place of worship I'd seen from the taxi on the way into town. Up close, the 133-year-old church looked in a sorry state. The large circular stained-glass windows that should equivalent of wearing a tie – you know, formal wear – so you might see office workers wearing them during the week. But everyone wears them on Sunday. If you're out tomorrow, you'll see."

After the second church service of the day, the family will go back home to eat the meal that was slowly cooking. Then they might have a nap because they got up so early that day. When the bells ring a third time, they get up and traipse back to church for another bout of fervent praising.

If the congregation is particularly unlucky, the minister might reel off a list of monetary contributions each member of the flock has made that week. Then they can return home. If the people of Tonga grow bored later in the afternoon, they can return to church a fourth time to practice singing, always an essential feature of Tongan church services.

"Wow, it sounds full on."

The waitress looked at me quizzically again.

"I mean, your whole Sunday is devoted to the church. You can't go shopping or watch a movie. All you can do is go to church."

"No, mostly we are with our families. We talk, tell stories and have some quality family time. But I love my church. The singing is amazing. If you get a chance, you should visit a church tomorrow and hear the singing for yourself."

Speaking of things to do the next day, I asked the waitress about the island I could visit.

"You mean Pangaimotu?"

"I think so."

"Well, it's beautiful; only a ten-minute boat ride from the wharf. It leaves at 10 am and 11 am. You pay fifty pa'anga ($20) and that includes a boat ride there and back, plus lunch. Everyone who goes there loves it. Take a snorkel if you go."

I thanked her for the information, ordered another Maka Lager and used a map to plot my route to the wharf the next morning. It looked straightforward.

10

I swept back the curtains to reveal a glorious South Pacific horizon of ocean and pigs. A collection of the trotters were out in the surf, snuffling as usual. From somewhere else came the distant sound of harmonised singing with a brass band accompaniment. I decided to investigate.

After breakfasting on some of the snacks I'd bought the previous day, I was outside, heading westwards. Instead of going to the Royal Palace, the coastal pathway was taking me in the opposite direction toward a church. Across the road was a man dressed in his Sunday best: a neatly pressed blue-and-white checked shirt and a long grey wrap-around sarong with a straw ta'avola tied around his waist, held in place with brown cord. He was carrying a small black book, perhaps a volume of hymns or a Bible. A short distance in front of him was a woman in a red dress with a longer ta'avola. She was holding a little girl's hand, who, instead of a ta'avola, wore a bright yellow dress. She looked like she was going to a party. I supposed she was: God's party.

The singing abruptly stopped and so did the brass band, only a stray tuba boomed solo for a second until it ceased its rumbling. The source of the now silent musicians and vocalists was a small but perfectly handsome white church with a light blue roof. The congregation was making their way in, joining the people already seated. I lingered outside, waiting for the singing to resume, but it looked like I had missed the pre-service rehearsal. Instead, the parishioners were engaged in hushed conversation. I decided to leave them to it.

Twenty minutes later, I was walking past the Royal Palace when suddenly I heard more singing which, when I turned a corner, swelled into a rich harmonised chorus of voices. If the clouds had parted and a large God-like finger appeared, then this was the exact soundtrack to accompany it. It was coming from another church up the road, this one much bigger, and I almost tripped over myself in my eagerness to witness the event.

The Centenary Chapel, otherwise called the King's Church, was large and perfectly white. Even from two hundred metres away, the singing sounded sublime: the most perfect mass of textured vocal I had heard in any church, including on TV. Cars were pulling up outside the church so that people (every last one of them dressed in their finery) could enter the cavernous, song-filled hall. Leading from the front was a man wearing a ta'avola, topped with a white shirt and jacket. As a bold addition, the gent sported a black bow tie. He swung his arms in a wave-like motion, commanding the flock to sing for the Lord. And sing they did; each and every one of them, making me wonder what happened to people who were tone deaf. Did they sing under their breaths, or mime? Were they banished to other, lesser churches? I did not know. But to me, it appeared that everyone in Tonga was born to sing.

Reluctantly, I had to leave: I had a boat to catch, and so left the church, passing through the empty streets of Nuku'alofa, not even a piglet or hound to keep me company for the thirty minutes it took to walk to the wharf. And when I got there, I found myself the only person in attendance. Thinking I had somehow gone wrong and ended up at the wrong place, I looked at my map just as a car pulled up, the first one I'd seen in a long while.

"You want to go to Pangaimotu?" asked the driver, a sumo-sized man.

I nodded, uncertainly. "I think so," I said, wondering if this was how it worked in Tonga. You show up at the wharf and a man in a station wagon drives up and offers you a ticket.

"The boat goes from over there." He pointed to a small covered seating area.

"Thanks."

"Boat will come soon."

"Thanks. Do I buy a ticket from you?"

The man looked at me in a funny way. "No. you buy it from the guy on the boat."

And with that, this Good Samaritan drove off, leaving me alone again. I walked over to the seating area and waited.

11

A few people eventually turned up, all of them foreigners. One was an older white man wearing a trilby and shorts. There was a young couple who sounded Australian and a trio of Chinese men. The biggest group were a foursome of thirty-something Kiwi men. They were also the noisiest of the bunch. But I had other things to contend with, namely the local man sitting beside me.

He was apparently not waiting for the boat and had been shuffling along the road when he had spotted our small crowd. He then made a beeline for me and was now staring at me with a gap-toothed mouth, sunken face and vacant eyes. Whether he was high on kava, booze or something else, I could not tell, but there was something not right about him.

"Where you goin'?" he mumbled.

"The island. I'm waiting for the boat."

He considered this, still staring at me. I tried to ignore him by looking at my phone.

"Where you goin'?" he asked again.

I repeated my answer, adding the actual name of the island.

The man lifted his legs and sat cross-legged on his perch beside me. He clearly wasn't going anywhere soon. I continued with my phone screen vigil as more people arrived: two middle-aged couples. They chatted by the water's edge.

"Where you goin'?" the man asked for the third time.

This time I ignored him.

"Where you goin'?"

Mentally gritting my teeth, I told him.

The man was silent for about one minute, occasionally snatching glances at the other assembled passengers. Perhaps he was going to bother one of them, I hoped.

"Where you goin'?"

That was it; I stood up and walked away. The man didn't like this and finally said something different from his usual refrain. "Why you ignorin' me, mate?"

I sat down further along, putting other people between us, hoping the boat would hurry up and arrive. The man in the trilby approached me. "Don't worry about him," he said in an Australian accent. "He's harmless. He's always hanging about here."

Mr Trilby was called Derek and he told me he'd retired to Tonga five year previously after his wife had died. Deciding to live somewhere quiet and uncrowded, he chose Tonga. "It's close enough that I can get back to Sydney if I need to, but far away enough that I can have some peace from all the crap back in Oz."

"So you own a house here? I thought only Tongans could do that?"

"I own the house but I only lease the land it's built on. It's a 99-year lease, but I'll be long gone before then."

I changed the subject. "Did you get caught up in the cyclone a few months back?"

"Absolutely. It was terrifying. The noise was unreal, like something from a disaster film. But my roof survived. It's funny; my roof is a hip roof, meaning all the slopes are quite gentle and go off at tangents. All the other houses in my neighbourhood with the same type of roof survived, too. But the houses with the gable roofs lost them." He looked out to sea. "I've heard another one's coming in a few days. It's already skimmed past Vanuatu."

I nodded. "Cyclone Keni."

"Yeah. But I think we're going to be okay. It's Fiji that'll take the brunt."

Just then, the small boat arrived: a small vessel that passengers were soon wobbling aboard. Derek told me to have a beer with him later on, and that he would tell me about the famous Tongan ladyboys."

"Ladyboys? I thought that was Thailand?"

"Not just Thailand; Tonga has them too. I'll tell you about them over a beer." And with that, he wandered off to speak to the young couple who I later learned were his daughter and her husband visiting Tonga for the week. I grabbed my hat and headed out to the vessel.

12

Pangaimotu came into view: a wedge of tightly-packed palm trees nestled above a line of yellow sand. If I were an Eighteenth-century pirate, I would be rejoicing at the sight: an island paradise within which to bury my treasure.

As we got closer, the sea turned from deep blue to a most pleasing turquoise, the stuff of holiday brochures, even though a brochure would probably not include the hulking and rusting hull of a shipwreck with its front half sticking out of the ocean as if raiders had scuttled it. The visible part of the wreck was full of gaping holes and yet someone had placed a Tongan flag on its prow. In a way, it looked great.

Once ashore, almost everyone splashed their way back into the water, swimming over to the wreck to look at the fish that had made it their home. The Kiwi men decided to hit the bar, as did Derek. As for me, I decided to be an explorer and set off walking around the island.

Just behind the bar area was a whole forest of broken trees: thick trunks that ended abruptly into snapped and snarled stubs. Others were toppled in entirety, uprooted by the storm that had passed in February. And yet, many trees had survived, perhaps aided by elasticity or just luck, and so I weaved around them, picking up spiky seeds underfoot which quickly encased my sandals and shorts. The seeds were so bothersome that I had to stand on one leg at a time to remove the most painful ones that became embedded between my toes. Then I emerged through the trees to find myself on a lonely, but beautiful stretch of beach, with the sand so narrow in parts, the ocean had engulfed it, forcing me to wade into warm water to carry on with my trek.

Ten minutes later, the beach widened and the mangroves thinned to reveal a thin estuarine river that was snaking its way through a forest of bent palm trees. I stopped for a moment, taken by the landscape. It was almost the same scene I had seen in childhood dinosaur movies. If a brachiosaurus stomped into view, it would have looked at home.

Further around the island, I came to a more substantial obstacle: a full fronded palm that had crashed and spilled into the ocean. Dead leaves had gathered within its carcass of branches. The barrier was so bulky and bothersome that I had to stop to think about things. One option was to turn around and retrace my steps. Two was to head into the Land that Time Forgot or, three, I could press on, weave my way around the felled palm and hope the water wasn't too deep.

I chose option three and waded into the ocean again, narrowly avoiding a large orange sea cucumber feeding in the gravelly shallow water. It was the size of my forearm but thicker by a measure. And then, when the water suddenly got deeper and the bottom of my shorts took a drenching, I began to regret my decision of carrying on. Maybe this was a bad idea, I felt, especially with a strong sea current looping around my sandaled feet. Plus, there was the possibility of sharks. That would be great, I thought, to be washed away and left floating in prime shark territory. I grabbed a twisted palm branch and pulled myself around the dead tree, thankful to find firm footing on the other side.

Back on dry land, I breathed a sigh of relief and realised I could hear voices. I was almost back to the start and was so thankful that I almost ran. Instead, I walked, as cool as a sea cucumber, into camp and only stopped when I reached the bar. I needed a beer after all the excitement.

13

Derek was sitting by himself at a table in the shade. He waved me over. His daughter was snorkelling somewhere with her husband and, to pass the time, Derek had drunk two pints of Tongan beer and was now on his third.

"So do you come here often?" I asked, taking a sip of my drink. It was delicious and I had to stop myself from swigging half the glass in one go. Beer tasted best on a hot tropical day, especially after dicing with death in shark-infested waters.

"I used to come most Sundays, but now I only come occasionally, like when I have people visiting. Mostly, I prefer to tend my garden."

"What about church? Do you ever go?"

"Sometimes. But I can't be bothered with all that, to be honest. But the singing's good. Have you heard it?"

I told him I had.

We both stared at the ocean for a while, silent in thought, watching as a young Chinese man climbed onto the broken ship hull and launched himself into the hypnotic water. And then we saw something unusual. Not far from the ship were a couple of bobbing heads. As they came closer to the shore, two people emerged from the water with sodden T-shirts. One was about twenty and the other was younger, but between them, they carried a large, flat-screen TV. Water sluiced from its sides as the pair nonchalantly waded up onto the sand, hauling it like water-borne removal men. Derek and I watched as they disappeared with their ocean cargo behind some huts.

"That was an unusual thing to see," I remarked.

Derek didn't comment, at least not at first; he was busy slurping a mouthful of beer down his neck. "Yep," he finally said.

I said, "I doubt it will work."

"Probably not, but they'll scavenge bits from it. I've seen the locals bring all sorts of things out from the ocean – things from passing ships. I've seen microwaves and kettles come out. Once I saw a couple of guys haul a washing machine out. But I was going to tell you about the ladyboys of Tonga, wasn't I?"

Derek told me that, unlike the ladyboys of South East Asia, the ladyboys of Tonga were actually men in almost every sense. None had gone under the knife to alter their birth sex and none plied their trade in girlie bars across town (which did not exist anyway). Instead, these *fakaleiti*, as they were known, which translated to 'like a girl', were simply men living as women.

"So they're like cross-dressers?"

"Not really. Not how you mean, anyway. Fakaleitis usually come about when parents want a daughter but only have sons. Instead of trying for a girl next time, the mother cuts her losses and turns the last baby boy into a girl."

"Turns?"

"She raises him as a daughter, you know, dresses him in girl's baby clothes, ribbons and all that. As he gets older, she trains him how to cook, clean, fix clothes and look after younger kids in the village. His aunts teach him how to apply makeup and how to wax his legs. I don't know what happens after puberty though; you've seen some of the men around here: I can't imagine any of them dressing up as women and passing it off, even with lipstick and heels." Derek chuckled at this image.

I took in this information. "And this still goes on?"

"Yeah."

"And the boys are happy for it to happen."

"Good question. I think so. There's no stigma attached. You've got to remember that the family unit is number one here. It's *everything* in Tongan society. So everyone is accepted in the family, no matter whether they're a man, woman or something in between."

When fakaleitis grew into adults, Derek told me, they often retained their feminine side, dressing as women and entering employment as cleaners, waitresses and hairdressers. Some even married straight men, though we both wondered how this worked in a country where homosexuality was against the law.

Derek said, "It's strange, I know. But from what I've heard and read, a man who sleeps with a fakaleiti is not gay because he sees his partner as a woman. I'm still trying to get my head around that one."

And so with thoughts of flat-screen TVs appearing from the ocean depths and men dressed as women who were not regarded as crossdressers or transgenders, I sipped my beer and then bought another after that.

14

In my room, after packing for another flight, I checked up on the news about Cyclone Keni. Fiji had taken a direct hit. Thousands of people were hunkered down in emergency shelters with floods and damaged buildings everywhere. However, forecasters predicted that Keni's passage southwards would be less blustery; she was running out of steam and in the next 48 hours would cease to be a cyclone any more.

As I checked my flight reservations and hotel bookings for the next day, I pondered Tonga, a country I had known next to nothing about before my arrival. But now I knew lots about this tiny South Pacific nation. I had learned about its fishing pigs and its royal bats. I had discovered that the nation was wallowing in the fat of mutton flaps and that some men dressed (and acted) as women but were not regarded as gay. But most of all I had discovered that instead of being a boring day of religious worship, Sunday in Tonga was a festival of singing and discovering electrical items at the bottom of the sea. All in all, Tonga had surprised me by how much was going on under its sleepy surface of tropical palm trees.

Top L-R: *The Cyclone-damaged Free Church of Tonga; People fishing out in the surf; One of the charming homes of downtown Nuku'alofa*
Middle L-R: *The Tongan Royal Tombs at sunset; The wreck at Pangaimotu Island*
Bottom L-R: *The Tongan Royal Palace; The fishing pigs of Tonga*

CHAPTER 6. AUCKLAND, NEW ZEALAND

Interesting fact: Auckland has over 50 volcanoes.

I had assumed that Auckland was named after aucks, the large squawking seabirds that frequented colder climes. In my head, I imagined a bearded explorer sighting this southern land and noticing colonies of the birds through his telescope. "Land ahoy," he might have possibly bellowed to his crewmates. "A land of aucks!"

Except, I was utterly wrong.

First of all, aucks do not exist in this world or any other; the actual spelling of the seabird is 'auk'. Secondly, auks live in the Northern Hemisphere, whereas New Zealand is firmly in the Southern. In actual fact, the city was named rather mundanely. As a thank-you gesture to a friend for reviving his flagging naval career, New Zealand's first governor, William Hobson, named Auckland after his pal's official British title, the Earl of Auckland. Nowadays, if you want to visit the original Auckland, you have to go to the North of England where there is a little village called West Auckland. If a person is fortunate, they might catch sight of an auk there.

Around 4 pm, my Air New Zealand flight began a descent over Auckland, the biggest city of my trip, not counting Brisbane at the start and Sydney at the end. With a population of 1.6 million, it was New Zealand's largest city; its centre of commerce, education and entertainment and yet was not its capital. And the reason for this was down to indecision.

At first, a small fishing town called Okiato was the capital of the new British colony. But when William Hobson swished into town in the 1840s, he deemed Okiato unfit for purpose and relocated the capital slightly further south to Auckland, citing its large harbour and easy access to arable land as major factors for the move. Grand buildings were thrown up, streets were paved, and Auckland thrived until somebody suggested moving the capital again. When Hobson asked why, they told him it was a matter of geography. Auckland was at the northern end of the North Island, which meant anyone on official business from the bottom of the South Island was forced to endure a long journey northward, followed by an arduous sea crossing, and then a third journey up the length of the North Island. It took days: a journey which then had to be repeated on the way back. Hobson agreed that this was something of a bind but when nobody could decide where a new capital should go, he threw down a pin in the middle of a New Zealand map and stared at the town nearest: that place was Wellington. That decided, all the government ministries packed their bags and moved south.

But rather like New York is to Washington DC or Sydney is to Canberra, Auckland remained the main gateway to this most southerly of South Pacific nations and therefore prospered despite losing out to Wellington in the capital city stakes. As I spied it from above, through dark grey rain clouds, it reminded me of cities in Northern Europe. But compared to Nuku'alofa, with its paltry population of around 24,000 people, Auckland was back to the real world of major highways, skyscrapers, expansive parks and expensive housing estates. We touched down with barely a squeak of the wheels and trundled to the terminal of Auckland International Airport, home of the angriest woman in the world.

2

The woman handled a small section of the airport concerned with passport scanners. She ruled it with snide comments and prime anger. I was waiting in a line that fed off towards the five e-scanners the woman ruled court over. I was behind four other people and had been waiting for some time. I could see that the cause of the delay was a series of touch-screen monitors on which passengers had to answer questions before the plastic doors would allow them entry into the passport scanning area. Suddenly, one of them was free.

"Move forward," the woman sniped at the person at the front of my line, an elderly Chinese man with nervous eyes. The man made no effort to move and instead looked blankly at the woman in charge. Perhaps he couldn't understand English. "Lane 4!" the woman barked, pointing in the direction of the lane.

I regarded the security official. She was about forty, with a uniform that meant she was to be obeyed. The Chinese man clutched his passport and moved forward uncertainly. He went to lane 1 and stood behind a woman at the touch-screen monitor.

Mrs Angry didn't like this turn of events one little bit. She marched over to the Chinese gentleman and led him by the arm to the correct lane. Then she gave the poor man a lot of instructions about what to do next. Before waiting to see if any of these orders had filtered through, she marched back to head of the queue and sighed. Then she noticed that lanes 1 and 3 were both empty and ordered the next two people forward. These people were also Chinese and were a married couple. They both toddled together to lane 1.

Mrs Angry flipped her lid. "Stop!" she hissed. "Only ONE person at ONE lane at ONE time!" Mrs Angry was now Mrs Pissed-Off. The couple understood what she wanted, though, which was good for them, and the husband (who I noticed was wearing Wellington boots for some reason) moved to his own lane. Meanwhile, the Chinese man at lane 4 who could not understand English was waving his arms to attract her attention. He could not fathom how to answer the questions on the touchscreen computer. Mrs Angry rushed over, muttering under her breath. And while this was going on, lane 5 became available which meant it was my turn at the Gates of Hell.

I calmly walked to the lane and answered the first question on the monitor, which asked me whether I was from one of the approved e-passport countries. I was and so I went to the next question. It asked whether I had anything to declare. I didn't and moved on to question three, which asked another straightforward question. Questions four, five and six were just as simple. Meanwhile, in the lane next to me, the Chinese man was being yelled at for not complying with the on-screen instructions.

I turned back to my screen, getting restless when the next question came up, the longest so far. It was a huge paragraph basically asking me whether I was a student, I just pressed no. Suddenly, a big red cross appeared on the screen and told me to start the process from the beginning. I made a sigh of my own and answered question one again, followed by question two and the others. When I responded to the question that asked whether I was a student, a big red cross appeared again.

Damn! I muttered. What a joke!

I now had three choices: none favourable. I could vault the scanning area and make a run for the exit. I could begin the questionnaire a third time or I could summon the dragon. I tightened my chest and raised my hand.

"What?" she barked upon her approach. She was red in the face.

"There's something wrong with this lane. It's not letting me through."

Some steam escaped from the woman's nostrils and I was sure I could smell sulphur. Even so, her voice came out measured and calm. "The machine works fine, sir."

"But it won't let me through."

"It will if you answer the questions correctly." Her tone was sharp.

"But I answered them correctly and it wouldn't let me throu—"

"Fine! Show me what you did."

The woman breathed impatiently as I answered the first few questions. She was stealing glances at other passengers, not able to stand delays on any of her lines. And then I got the student question and, as I pressed no, the dragon could hold her fire no longer. "NO!" she screamed, causing everyone in the vicinity to look. "WHY DID YOU PRESS NO?"

"Because I'm not a student." My pulse was racing and I didn't like the fact I was suddenly the centre of attention inside Auckland International Airport. I could not risk being deported because then I would miss my flight to Samoa.

"But what about the rest of the question?" The woman was hissing now. Or fizzing.

I looked at her blankly.

"You didn't read it, did you?"

I thought about how to answer this and simply shook my head like the bad dog I was.

"*Jesus!*" The woman rubbed her head. "If you'd read the question, it asked whether you were an international student, which you're probably not, or whether you're a tourist visiting for less than three months, which you might be. Are you any of those things?"

I admitted I was.

"So why did you press no?"

"I don't know."

"I do. It's 'cos you thought you were too smart to read the whole question." She gave me a withering look that was reserved for simpletons and instead of dousing me in flame, she doused me in nasty words. "Ignorant people annoy me so much."

I answered the questions for the third time and this time entered the passport scanner. And then I entered the sixth nation of my trip. Welcome to New Zealand a sign read. Yes, some welcome.

3

Auckland was ridiculously expensive, one of the most expensive cities I had ever visited. I was glad I was only going to be in the city for two nights because any longer than that and I'd have to take out a bank loan or take to wearing a balaclava. In one small convenience store, I picked up a small bottle of water and was astonished when the man behind the counter scanned it and asked for six dollars.

"Six dollars?" I said. "I thought it was just water."

"It is."

I handed over the money and as I was about to leave noticed the shopkeeper grinning. "Like the look, mate. Very pink." He grinned some more. It wasn't a nice grin.

I looked down and could see what he meant. By some strange twist of misfortune, and one I had not realised until this very moment, I was dressed in pink.

Twenty minutes previously, I had checked into the hotel, had a shower and thrown on some clean clothes. I should have glanced at myself in the mirror before stepping outside. My shorts were pink, my T-shirt was pink and now my face was pink. I could not believe I had done such a thing and suddenly felt self-conscious.

The man now had a wry smile on his face. "You look…interesting," he said, establishing himself as the most sarcastic person in Auckland.

I fled his establishment, keenly aware I was walking around in pink clothes like I was making a fashion statement. What made it worse was that it was so bloody cold. Unlike Fiji and Tonga, where T-shirts and shorts had been my apparel of choice, the weather in Auckland was like autumn in Britain: cold, windy and drizzly. And it seemed to have suddenly changed because when I'd entered the shop, it was fairly warm. But now, standing out like a sore pink thumb with goose pimples on my arms, I looked like a mental patient who has escaped the hospital. I hurried back to the hotel to change into something more becoming, and to get my coat.

Back outside, I realised that Auckland was about as cosmopolitan as anywhere I had ever visited. If I took a photo of the people wandering the town centre and showed it to people back home, most of them would be nonplussed where it was taken. I could have been in Tokyo, Shanghai, Paris or even Delhi. In a 2013 census, it was found that almost a third of Auckland's population was born in another country, most of them England, China or India

I wandered down a hill populated by shops selling lottery tickets, a 7-Eleven, a photo restoration outlet and a series of cheap restaurants advertising Mexican, Turkish and Italian food. I carried on past the eateries and came to a busy intersection where I spied a giant owl. The big blue bird with orange feet and green wings was sitting on a large pedestal and was about as tall as I was. It was staring at me with huge, dinner-plate yellow eyes. A placard at the owl's base told me it was one of 47 birds placed in the city, sometimes inside shopping centres or cinema complexes and even libraries. Mostly though, they were simply out in the street like this one

The owls were all part of a project called the Haier Big Hoot, a children's charity foundation who had arranged for local artists to take delivery of bare, white, unpainted owls with which to adorn their own colour designs and flourishes. This meant that every single owl was bespoke. In a month or so, the flock would be rounded up and put into a charity auction. What a great idea, I thought.

I passed by the harbour and the grand sandstone home of the Auckland Ferry Terminal, an Edwardian-era building that was one of the most prominent structures there. It led to a pier and then a gift shop that sold more souvenirs than I'd seen on my entire trip so far. After picking up a fridge magnet, I was off again, marvelling at the city skyline now that the lights were coming on. Jutting above everything was the magnificent Sky Tower, the tallest structure in the Southern Hemisphere. The next day, I intended to visit it, but for now, with the cold southern wind biting at my neck, I headed back to the hotel.

4

The next morning was raining so heavily I remained in the hotel. After lunch, things calmed down and I was back by the harbour for a boat tour. Because the sea looked choppy and the clouds were thick with grey, I was one of only a few passengers to join the ninety minute-long tour and the only one to sit outside on the back deck. Within a minute of setting off from the Captain Cook Wharf, I was being bombarded by water-spray and attacked by a ferocious wind that had me seeking refuge behind a supporting beam.

From my rear seat, I watched the city skyline receding, helped by a great swirl of dark grey stratus rendering the top reaches of the Sky Tower invisible. After passing a colossal cargo ship docked at the commercial wharf, we headed into open water past a frail-looking structure jutting out of the sea on thin wooden legs. I tuned into the narration coming from the speaker system.

"This is the Bean Rock Lighthouse," the voice told me. "In 1871, it cost three thousand pounds to build. Although you can't really tell from here, it's hexagonal in shape."

Not only didn't it look hexagonal, it didn't look like a regular lighthouse full stop, partly because it was in the middle of the sea, but also because of its spindly look. Lighthouses were usually solid things, perched on cliff faces, built to withstand the elements. This one looked like it would blow away with one swirl of a gale.

"When the first lighthouse keeper, a man called Hugh Brown, moved in," the voice said, "he arrived by rowing boat and lived in the top part of the lighthouse, which had a kitchen, a bedroom, a living area and a long-drop toilet that went straight into the sea."

Nice, I thought.

"But he must have thought it was okay because he stayed for nineteen years, occasionally getting visits from his family. When there was an emergency, he would flash a Morse code signal from a torch and hoped someone was looking. For people on the mainland, if they owned a good pair of binoculars, and if the day was clear, they might have seen Mr Brown jogging the circumference of the lighthouse's outside veranda, which took him 35 paces, start to finish."

What sort of person becomes a lighthouse keeper, I pondered, especially on a lighthouse accessible only by boat? To live in isolation, battered by waves and then have to bare nether regions to seagulls and spray: it seemed the pastime of the unhinged, particularly when factoring in the lack of entertainment.

By 1912, the need for a resident keeper was redundant due to the installation of an automatic light. And, as the decades passed, the old lighthouse fell into disrepair. By 1985, it was a shell of its former self and was pulled from the sea, taken ashore and restored. And then it was replaced: a reminder of a simpler time gone by.

By now the rain was lashing down harder and a woman came to check I was all right. She was wearing a boat tour windbreaker, and when I told her I was fine, she said she would bring me a warm drink soon. Maybe I was more like the old lighthouse keepers than I thought, preferring solitude and rain to the company of others. But to be honest, the main reason I had seated myself away from everyone else was that they were all either couples or families with kids. The last thing they needed was a bloke from England intruding on their conversations to tell them about the hermaphrodite pigs of Vanuatu or the ladyboys of Tonga.

We continued our stormy voyage past a large island which looked suspiciously like a volcano, which was precisely what it was. Rangitoto Island was a dormant volcano that had formed six hundred years ago, in dramatic fashion, to create the island at which I was now staring. When the British arrived in the 1850s, they bought the island for the princely sum of fifteen pounds and used it as a source of basalt as well as a stopping point to dry out drunken sailors. Behind it, lightning flashed, followed by a thunderous roar. I could hold out no longer; with the rain coming down heavier than ever, I went inside where I loitered at the back of the cabin.

The speaker intoned: "The name of the volcano is Maori for 'Bleeding Sky' and if any of you are wondering whether it might erupt during your stay in Auckland, then let me reassure you that it might." While we digested this potentially life-threatening nugget of information, the voice explained that a few years ago some scientists armed with a big drill and collecting tins had driven a 150m hole into the volcano to retrieve samples. When they had enough rock, they took it back to their laboratories, rubbed their chins for a bit and stared at the graphs. It told them that, although the volcano had been quiet for close to six centuries, it was not yet extinct; it could erupt at any moment. But, if and when it did, they calculated that the resulting firework show would not compromise the safety of any Aucklanders. For a start, no one lived on the island and, second, Rangitoto was surrounded by water, which was where most the lava would end up. One civil defence official even stated that if it did explode, instead of being something to run away from, it would be 'something nice to look at'.

We powered away from the volcano that could blow at any moment and headed into a fierce storm. Water sluiced across the deck and rain flew horizontally past the side of the boat. And then we passed under the Auckland Harbour Bridge, which, unlike its more famous namesake in Sydney, looked nothing special: just a standard bridge with a small arch in the middle. As it faded behind us, and the city came into view again, I was thankful when the woman from earlier brought me a cup of tea and a slice of cake, but less pleased when a wave rocked my drink onto the already slick deck. As I chomped on my banana muffin, I wondered whether anyone had ever died from a volcano while eating a slice of cake.

5

Back on dry land, the sun came out, banishing the drizzle but not the wind. If anything, the wind was worse, which worried me because the next afternoon I was due to fly to Samoa. But there was no point worrying about that; so I took a photograph of an old steamboat instead. It was long and black with a jolly yellow chimney jutting up from its middle section. On the side, someone had painted its name:

the William C Daldy. In times gone by, the William C Daldy was a tugboat. It arrived in Auckland in 1936, all the way from Scotland.

Looking at the boat, I wondered how it had managed to make the voyage – after all, it was so small. But the boat had done it, making the journey from Glasgow to New Zealand, powered by coal all the way.

And what a journey it must have been. After heading past France and Spain and calling at Algiers and Port Said in Egypt, the little tug made a transit through the Suez Canal to make landfall in Yemen, Sri Lanka, Jakarta and Australia before the final chug into New Zealand, 81 days later.

More or less from day one, the William C Daldy (named after Auckland Harbour's first chairman), chugged around the harbour towing boats and occasionally making rescue runs: a useful but largely uninteresting life. That all changed in 1958 when the tug hit the big time. 1958 was the year that saw the construction of the Auckland Harbour Bridge and, as the central section was being manoeuvred into place by barges, a storm raged, threatening to blow the pieces away. For 36 hours, the Daldy held the middle part in place by using its powerful engines and tugging ropes. When the storm passed, the central bridge section had survived and was moved into position as the old tugboat returned to port for a well-deserved rest.

But then the Daldy grew old. A younger, more agile, model came on the scene, swishing her sleek lines and freshly-painted deck at the old timer. And so, in 1977, the old tug was retired, most probably headed for the scrap yard. But then, something quite amazing happened: a set of upstanding Aucklanders bought the boat and, with the help of wealthy sponsors, set about restoring her. Three years later, she was back out, steaming across the harbour in her new guise as a pleasure boat. Today, she still uses her original coal boilers and is staffed by a collection of qualified volunteers.

A fantastic tale, I think you'll agree.

6

Auckland's impressive skyline is dominated by the Sky Tower, a concrete and steel communication tower that emits radio signals across the city day and night.

I stared up at it, wondering whether I should bungee jump from the top. For $225, I could launch myself from the apex, plummet for eleven seconds and then dangle lifelessly after my heart attack. No, I had never done a bungee jump in my life and wasn't about to start with one in Auckland. Besides, the jumps were cancelled for the day due to high winds. Instead, I paid a hefty sum to ride a lift to the viewing platform on the 51st floor.

I clutched my ticket and headed toward the roped-off line that fed to the elevator doors. Just ahead of me was a Japanese gentleman who was also a solo traveller. Before we reached the beginning of the line, a man with a camera shouted something at me. "Stand there," he said, pointing at a screen. I did so and so did the Japanese man. I looked at him and he looked at me. He bowed and then so did I. It was all a bit embarrassing.

"Closer together please," the man with the camera asked, gesturing with his hands. He clearly thought we were a couple. If I'd still been in my pink clothes, I could have understood. He glanced my way. "Don't be shy. Maybe put your arm around him, sir."

Both the Japanese man and I realised what was happening and instead of moving together to hold hands and kiss, we moved apart and explained to the buffoon with the camera that we didn't even know each other.

"Oh my God, I'm so sorry," the photographer gushed. "I just thought…" His voice trailed off. "Well, just stand separately and I'll take photos individually."

I told him I wasn't bothered about a photo, which was true. Why would I want to pay for a photograph of me superimposed onto a background of Auckland's skyline? No thanks. But the Japanese man was more amenable and stayed put.

The view from the top was great: a 360-degree view of the city and its surrounds. The harbour and the harbour bridge were visible, as were lines of jetties where almost two thousand expensive yachts lay moored. Closer inland was a forest of downtown skyscrapers. Auckland was definitely a city on the up and up.

After doing a full circle, I braved the 'walk of terror' across some extra-reinforced, transparent, glass panels, and then realised that the tower was swaying due to the high winds aloft. It was a most surreal experience to feel drunk when completely sober. The designers of the Sky Tower had built it to cope with winds of up 120 mph, where it can merrily sway up to a metre side-to-side, rather like a flower blowing in the breeze. Not only that, since New Zealand is prone to tremors, the tower can survive an earthquake of up to 8.0 magnitude, which was higher than any earthquake ever recorded in the country.

I went to the Sky Tower Bar, almost backing out at the last second when I saw the price for a small bottle of beer, but thought, what the heck, I was never coming back. I took my drink to a spare section of the window and stared out across the most southerly city of my trip. Auckland had been okay, but not somewhere I would ever want to rush back too. The main problem was it was like any other big city in the Western world: perfectly nice, often expensive but a little bit boring. But Auckland was never meant to be one of the main draws on my Pacific tour; instead, it was a transit point between Tonga and Samoa. Speaking of which: I stared towards the northeast. Somewhere out there, almost two thousand kilometres distant, was my next port of call: Samoa.

Top L-R: *Downtown Auckland, as seen from the observation deck of the TV Tower; Me suddenly facing some colder weather in New Zealand*
Middle L-R: *The TV tower lit up at night; One of the painted owls, part of the Haier Big Hoot project*
Bottom L-R: *The Bean Rock Lighthouse; View of Auckland from my harbour boat trip*

Chapter 7. Apia, Samoa

Interesting fact: More Samoans live outside Samoa than in (mainly in Australia, New Zealand and the USA).

The wind was wreaking havoc with flights in an out of Auckland International Airport. The previous evening, as I had traipsed back to the hotel after my farewell meal, the wind had forced me to hunch my shoulders and walk at a marked angle. Litter blew past me like it was escaping a hole in a plane. Later, thunder and lightning boomed and flashed as a howling gale battered my hotel window.

According to the news, the late night winds had roared at over 100km/h, lashing down torrents as they scoured the city. At first, I had thought it was Keni making an appearance after chasing me around the South Pacific for a week, but it was another storm, this one nameless. By the time the tempest had moved on, detritus had blocked roads, thousands were left without power and there were floods everywhere.

As I drove to the airport, I could see for myself the after-effects of the storm: upturned wheelie bins, snapped branches and, at one point, a smashed car window. The number of leaves on the ground was staggering, as if someone had picked them off ten thousand trees and brushed them all over the roads, pavements and parks. And though the weather was now calm, I knew that flight delays were going to be a high probability, which turned out to be the case. Instead of a leisurely afternoon flight that would have got me to Samoa at 8.35pm, my flight was delayed by four hours. I was just thankful my plane was leaving; other people were not so lucky. The list of flight cancellations and diversions was causing scenes of panic at the airport. So, instead of wallowing in self-pity, I decided to use my free meal voucher to do something I had never done before; something truly disgusting and horrid.

I bought a McDonald's meal and, taking a cue from Vanuatu's forward-thinking plastic policy, I handed back the straw. Then I sat down at an empty table. The table next to me was pushed up against mine but was free of people but full of rubbish. Whoever had been sitting there had not bothered to clean up. A tray of greasy chicken bones and crumpled serviettes lay there, and I shook my head at the boars who had left the table in that state. Then, like all solo travellers, I forgot all about the mess and removed the phone from my pocket and began browsing the internet, absently eating my salty fries. I got into a story about the storm. One unfortunate woman had been in driving when a tree toppled onto her car. She managed to stop but was trapped inside her vehicle, nursing serious injuries. She ended up in hospital, though the article did not specify how bad the injuries were.

I picked up my drink and took a slurp, continuing to read about the storm. It appeared that the local authorities were taking a lot of flak because they had done little to warn the population about the incoming winds. And then I took another slurp through the straw and stopped reading mid-sentence.

A straw?

I didn't have a straw.

And then the full horror struck me dumb. Inadvertently, I had picked up the discarded drink next to me to take full-bodied slurps. Feeling numb, I placed the Coke on the next table, wiping my mouth and inwardly gagging. I looked at the chicken bones and the sachets of open mayonnaise packets and gagged again. I imagined some double-chinned, greasy-mouthed oaf slurping away before me, possibly spitting grease back down his straw, I imagined him sucking up his Coca-Cola, burping and then sending the liquid back down to bubble and fester with untold bacteria. I looked around to see if anyone had witnessed the terrible event, but none had. I grimaced again and shook my head at the unfairness of it all. I had gone my whole life without doing this, and now, here in Auckland, I had done the unspeakable, not just once, but twice. If someone had offered me a thousand pounds to do what I'd just done, I would have refused. I felt ill with disgust; sullied to my core. With my appetite gone, I collected up my rubbish and tossed it into the bin. Auckland would always have a bad taste for me.

2

The four-hour flight north to Samoa wasn't too bad. I especially liked the Air New Zealand touchscreen facility that allowed me to place an order and pay for a glass of wine from the comfort of my seat rather than having to wait for the trolley to come past. Press the button, swipe my credit card and two minutes later a member of the cabin crew served me a drink.

We eventually landed at midnight, at a point in the Pacific Ocean about halfway between New Zealand and Hawaii. But midnight is never a good time to arrive in a new country, especially with a wine-induced thirst raging at my throat. As I shuffled forward to get my passport stamped, all I could think about was buying some water from a shop outside. Except, there were no shops, especially at quarter past midnight. Instead, I followed a man, who had been waiting for me, towards his minibus, grimly realising that if I had that dirty Coke drink with me now, I would swig the lot with relish, chicken fat and all.

"Just waiting for two more people," said the driver.

"Two more? To the same hotel?"

"Yeah."

Bugger, I lamented. I had presumed my airport transfer would be a private one. While the driver wandered off to the terminal to collect them, I wallowed in the shadows of the back seat of a minibus to dream of liquid. And then I remembered I had a can of Tongan beer tucked away in my suitcase. It would be warm but drinkable and, in the absence of a shop selling water, it would have to suffice. I opened the sliding door, stepped into the humid night air and walked to the back of the minibus. After opening the hatch, I rummaged in my luggage like a demented man until I felt the shape of the can in my hand. And then I zipped up the bag, closed the hatch and re-entered the vehicle.

The taste of the warm beer was like nectar. I drained half the can in one go, letting out a satisfying belch of a seasoned ale drinker. And then the other passengers appeared: a young couple walking towards the minibus with the driver. It left me in a quandary. Should I drain the rest of the can and risk a gas explosion in my innards or wait it out and drink it en route. The problem was, though, they would think I was an alcoholic, not capable of holding off the booze until I got to the hotel. So I decided to hide the can, grasping it below seat level. I would try to swig the rest of the can on the journey, hopefully under cover of darkness.

The Kiwi couple sat in the row in front of me, which would make my secret beer swilling easier. But what I didn't count on were the bumpy roads and the intermittent lights. Every time I raised the can of beer to attempt a guzzling, either we could bump over something or a streetlight would illuminate my subterfuge. Aiding and abetting the misery was the driver who, periodically, would stare at me in his mirror, as if daring me to drink Tongan beer in Samoa. Five minutes later, I timed a slurp well, but then, in my haste to remove the can undercover, I squeezed it too much, which resulted in an audible and unmistakable can-squeezing sound. The woman ahead of me turned around. The whole minibus probably smelt of beer and so I smiled and held in a burp.

"Hi," she said.

"Hi," I said, teeth clenched to retain the odour of Tongan beer.

"Hi," her boyfriend said. The question of beer hung in the air unless I was paranoid, which I probably was.

I was still gripping the infernal can. It was swishing about with the motion of the minibus and my fingers were becoming slippery with sweat. The woman told me that they had never been to any other country outside of New Zealand until now. "We're excited, but pity about the flight delay, eh? That was a bummer."

"Yeah, but you can't help the wind. At least we got here." I was like a ventriloquist dummy.

The man decided to speak. "My brother and his wife came here last year. They said it was amazing. We're going to hire some mopeds in a couple of days so we can see the island. We'll probably visit the blowholes and the caves. You're welcome to join us if you want?"

I was taken aback by the invitation. Little did they know I was a beer-swilling monster who drank from other people's straws in my spare time. "Oh, wow, thanks for the offer, but I'm only here for a couple of days. Then I'm off to Sydney."

Despite the dark, I could see the couple were shocked. "Only two days?" the young man said. "That seems a bit extreme. You're hardcore, mate."

I thanked him for that but thought it perhaps wasn't a compliment. The rest of the journey passed in relative quiet, only the humming of the engine and the occasional change of gear to relieve the monotony of seeing nothing outside. And then we arrived at the hotel and I managed to manipulate the quarter-full can of beer into my knee pocket. It bulged alarmingly but at least it was semi-hidden. By the time I had got to my room, it had more or less emptied itself down my leg.

What a palaver. I went to bed troubled by the lateness of our arrival as well as the fact that my trip was almost at an end. Just Samoa and then a sneaky little side trip to East Timor and then I would be done and dusted.

3

As is often the case, a sunny morning in a new land has the power to cleanse the soul and remove any angst from the previous night. I was up early on my only full day in Samoa and intended to get out and explore as soon as I could. But breakfast delayed me due to a newspaper called the Samoa Observer. It led with the headline: Public Oppose New Chicken Tax.

Wacky headlines such as this brightened my mood further and I read the story with interest, sipping my insipid coffee. The main gist was the unfairness of the recently imposed tariff on imported chicken. It would, the report suggested, unjustly affect low and middle-income citizens of Samoa because chicken was the only meat they could afford. The story scoffed at the government's flimsy excuse for increasing the price of chicken: that they were worried about the negative health impact when people ate too much of it. The writer of the report wrote that the real reason was yet another underhanded money-making scheme thought up by politicians to fleece Samoans who could afford it least. To back up the point, the report featured interviews with five members of the public, asking them of their opinion.

Unsurprisingly, most of the interviewees thought the chicken tax was a bad idea, saying that if the price of chicken was going up, then their wages ought to go up too. A reasonable response came from an old gent called Waldell. He claimed he had been eating chicken for six decades and hadn't suffered any ill health because of it. Another man, whose photograph made him seem as if he was in disguise (large floppy hat and sunglasses) said he didn't even know about the tax and that it wouldn't affect him anyway. I suspected he worked for the government but wanted to conceal his identity. The article did not offer any official government statement; perhaps because they were too busy tucking into a chicken barbecue.

What the report failed to mention was that it wasn't just imported chicken affected by the price increase, it was also the infamous mutton flaps and turkey tails: low-grade foodstuff that the people of Samoa and Tonga seemed to love. It also didn't mention that homegrown chickens were exempt from the tax. Like other Pacific nations, Samoa is suffering from a health epidemic where nine out of every ten people are overweight or obese. So perhaps the government ought to be commended for the tax.

4

My hotel was in a good spot, right in the centre of the capital, Apia. Just across from it was the ocean and, in between, a little park known as the Sogi Recreational Area. A group of young men, none of whom looked overweight, were kicking a football around, their teams differentiated by whether they were wearing caps or not. A raised seawall bordered the ocean, the favoured hangout of small yellow fiddler crabs. The males had two claws, one much larger than the other that they used for fighting off other males or for attracting females. They looked like they were waving at me while running for cover.

As the wall curved off to the left, away from the recreational ground and into the town itself, there was an outdoor bus station, a busy place where a couple of dozen Nissan and Toyota buses with open side windows waited for passengers. People milled around them, some with bags slung over the backs, waiting to board. A couple of vendors walked between the buses with trays of drinks and snacks balanced on their shoulders.

The buses reminded me a little of American school buses, except older versions. Instead of being yellow, Apia's buses featured different designs, some highlighting tropical scenes, others of painted girls with flowers in their hair. One bus was called the Good Fortune, decked out in yellow and green, another, the Lady Trinity, favoured white and blue, but my favourite was a bright orange bus with a sky blue roof; the word Storm Express emblazoned on its side.

Behind the buses was a series of stalls. Each was protected from the elements by flimsy sheets of plastic stretched across metal frames. They were selling cold drinks, bagged-up fruit, T-shirts and washing powder. Further along was fish market where bored men and women sat reading from mobile phones as they swished away flies with leafy branches. Through the other side, I saw a man drinking a can of Coke and, as I watched, he tossed it into the ocean. Just like that: he threw his trash into the tropical water of the Pacific Ocean: his home, his paradise, despoiled by his action.

I couldn't believe the thoughtlessness of the man. I tutted in his direction but I don't think he even noticed. I looked where he had thrown the can and saw it had lodged itself between two large rocks. It wasn't alone. Three other cans, together with six Styrofoam cups lay there, plus a couple of plastic bottles. In the ocean, another can bobbed. It looked disgusting and I could not believe that the inhabitants of such a gorgeous tropical island could pollute their own waters in such a callous way.

Like a lot of Pacific nations, Samoa has a problem with plastic. The problem is threefold: the lack of recycling facilities, the amount of plastic packaging imported from abroad and a population so unused to sorting plastic for recycling that they just throw it away for someone else to deal with. In a sample carried out a few years ago, 97% of fish caught in Samoan waters had plastic in their stomachs. Unlike Vanuatu, Samoa is at a loss with what to do with its single-use plastic items, and the net result was a litterbin forming along its palm edged coastline.

5

When Europeans began their expansion into the Pacific region in the Eighteenth century, America and Germany set their sights on Samoa, then known as the Navigator Islands. The British were sniffing around too and, for a short while, all three conducted their business around each other, on different sections of the islands. Then the Germans got too big for their boots and began cultivating massive rubber and coconut plantations. In response, the Americans started ganging up with the locals to throw them out. The British, pottering around in Apia drinking tea and gin, watched the build-up of tension and pondered.

Things came to a head in 1889 when three German warships and three American warships had a stand-off in Apia harbour. The British put down their teacups and sent a boat out too. For a few months, all seven boats eyed each other like they were in a Spaghetti Western, none daring to do anything lest the others get the wrong idea and start a fight. As the stand-off rumbled into another month, war seemed imminent. Then, just as things were hotting up, a cyclone roared into the scene. Neither the Germans nor the Americans wanted to lose face by fleeing first and so all seven boats remained where they were, horribly exposed should the cyclone be a direct hit. Predictably, it was, and all boats apart from the British one sank, killing 135 people from both sides. With the flames of war doused, all three nations met to speak rationally and decided that the best course of action was to split the islands into two separate spheres of interest. Germany got the main island, which it called German Samoa; America got the other big one: American Samoa. The British gave up all their rights to Samoa in return for Tonga and some of the Solomon Islands. And this was how things stayed until the First World War when New Zealand came packing heat and kicked the Germans out. The Kiwis brought something else, too: influenza, which I'll be coming back to later.

6

In the centre of Apia lies a clock tower. It stands in the middle of a small roundabout, proud and tall. It is decked out in white and yellow with a pointy section at the top that features a clock on all four sides. Built in the 1920s, it serves as a memorial to Samoan servicemen who fought in the First World War. But, as well as acting as a totem of remembrance, Apia's clock tower once served as a focal point for time travel.

Before December 2011, Western Samoa and American Samoa operated at the far eastern fringes of the International Date Line. When it was Friday lunchtime in Western Samoa (Samoa's name prior to 1997), it was already Saturday afternoon in Australia and New Zealand. This made trade awkward. Even worse, while Samoans were attending Sunday church services, business was already being conducted in Sydney and Auckland in which Samoan companies could not take part. Effectively, Samoa was losing two days of trade, as well as the weekend, every seven days. Things had to change.

Some clever people sat in a room and scratched their heads until they had hatched a plan. It was simple in its ingenuity and when they shared their proposal with the population of Western Samoa, everyone cheered. Over in American Samoa, they booed; they wanted to stay as they were. On 29th December 2011, a crowd gathered around the clock tower in downtown Apia and awaited the stroke of midnight. When it chimed, they missed out on December 30th and jumped straight to New Year's Eve, skipping westwards over the International Date Line. Instead of being 21 hours behind Sydney, they were now four hours ahead. Instead of being one of the last places to see a day's sunset, they were now one of the first to see the sunrise. When TV cameras screened the first New Year celebrations of 2012, they showed Samoan fireworks first. Job done, the Samoans sat back and went to sleep for a while. Meanwhile, over in American Samoa, it was still the day before.

The distance between Apia, Samoa's capital, and Pago Pago, American Samoa's capital, is 93 miles and yet it has a flight time of one day. This is hard to get your head around. When a flight takes off at 8.30 in the morning from Samoa, it will land in Pago Pago at 7.55am the day before it left. Yes, the day before! You will arrive yesterday, which is a time travelling escapade worthy of a novel. Where has a whole day gone; after all, the physical journey only took 35 minutes? It's gone nowhere – it's still heading towards you the next day, I think. And if you fly in the other direction, leaving

American Samoa at 4.45pm, you will land in the other Samoa at 6.20pm the next day. People are always missing their flights or missing their connections due to the pesky International Date Line quirk.

Opposite the clock tower was a grand white building, which in most towns would be a museum or perhaps an administrative building, but in Apia was the Chow Mow & Co Ltd building, a Chinese-owned supermarket and department store that a group of Australians had built in the 1920s before selling it thirty years later. Signs on the window said it was selling 4G SIM cards as well as household goods. I walked past it, keeping to the shade offered by the store's arched walkway, passing the Samoa Post Office, a nondescript building that sat above a small shopping precinct. A few people were going in but, by and large, downtown Apia was free of crowds.

Across the road was something more eye-catching: the six-story Central Bank of Samoa, the issuer of the funky Samoan tala, surely one of the most colourful sets of banknotes in the world. But the bank was no slouch to colour either because it was adorned in blues and pinks; finished with a dazzling array of what looked like red fire poles running vertically around its side. Next to it, like a gigantic, oversized brother, was one of the tallest buildings in Samoa, the eight-storey Government Building, which looked like a large hotel, except for the bulbous maroon dome on the top that represented a traditional Samoan meeting house.

Meeting houses are important in Samoa. Before European colonisation, Samoa was ruled by a traditional set of values known as the *Fa'amatai* system. Individual chiefs governed large villages, looking after the welfare, finances, and marriages of the people who lived in them. They were also responsible for dealing with any issues of crime or any points of village law. These chiefs, or *matai*, held court in meeting houses: large oval (or sometimes round) open-plan structures with wooden posts that held up a domed, thatched roof. And though the concept of these village chiefs has diminished slightly, elders and their meeting houses still exist all over Samoa. In Apia, almost all members of Samoa's parliament are made up of village chiefs, which explained the meeting house dome on top of the Government Building. Just behind the large building was an actual meeting house. I traipsed along a path full of skinks to see it.

Instead of a thatched roof, its upper reaches were of metal, a prudent move in a country frequently visited by cyclones. The meeting house's concrete and brick base was about a metre off the ground (to keep it free from floods, serpents and creepy-crawlies, I presumed), with about forty wooden posts spread around its circumference holding up the roof. I walked along its perimeter wondering what essential decisions Samoan elders had made there. Important ones, probably. With a free-flowing sea breeze, it seemed a good place in which to discuss serious matters. And speaking of serious matters, I decided it was time to get some breakfast.

7

The most westerly McDonald's restaurant on Planet Earth is in Apia. Or was it the most easterly? I could not get my brain to accept which one. When the restaurant was built, Samoa had not crossed over the International Date Line. Back then, Apia's McDonald's was definitely the most westerly, but since crossing over the date line, surely it ought to be most easterly? A man in the hotel told me it was the most easterly, but an up-to-date travel website said it was the most Westerly. Whichever it was, in need of sustenance, I decided to seek it out and order a Sausage McMuffin in either the most westerly or easterly MacDonald's in the world.

To get to it, I had to walk through downtown Apia, which, instead of looking distinctly Samoan, resembled a small-time Australian town. Nothing was particularly high rise or old-looking, but neither were any of the shops, stores and cafes particularly interesting. The town was fairly busy, with more pedestrians than earlier and most looked overweight. But none seemed particularly unhealthy as they strolled around in T-shirts and flip-flops. Some men wore suits and many older women preferred long flowery dresses.

I took a detour through the snazzily-titled SNPF Plaza, a hotbed of souvenir stores, clothes emporiums and food stalls. It was here that I saw something I liked: flowers. Many of Apia's womenfolk were wearing large flower decorations in their hair called a *sei*. They wore them behind their ears as part of a hair tie. Behind the right ear meant the woman was single; behind the left, she was taken. One woman had a flower on both sides, which gave me cause for concern. But each flower looked great – whether bright yellow, vivid scarlet or simple blue or white – they made each wearer looked truly tropical. After finding nothing else of interest, I exited the plaza and walked past a surf shop, a Bluebird Lumber and Hardware shop and then a taxi rank. Then I spied the golden arches of MacDonald's. It seemed to be under renovation, but was still open and packed with burger-loving punters. Even at 10.30 in the morning, burgers were going down a treat, and I scanned the menu for anything that contained mutton flaps but could only see regular fare. With my breakfast meal, I sat down and availed myself of the free MacDonald's Wi-Fi to read the latest news on Cyclone Keni.

As I knew, Fiji had taken the brunt. But the reports were more detailed now. Trees had been uprooted, boats overturned and Queen's Road, the main strip in Nadi, was flooded. Nine people died and thousands were still living in emergency shelters. According to the news, Fiji was now basking in sunshine as its people cleared up the mess. As for Keni, as predicted, it dissipated before reaching Tonga.

I switched websites to search for things to do in Apia and discovered there was a couple of churches and the Sheraton hotel. The Sheraton was worth seeing due to its history and architecture. There was also Robert Louis Stevenson's former home. This made me pause for thought: was this the same Robert Louis Stevens I knew about – the famous Scottish writer of *Treasure Island* and the *Strange Case of Dr Jekyll and Mr Hyde*? Yes, it damned well was.

As well as writing novels, Stevenson had been something of a traveller, possibly due to a chest problem which he believed was made worse by living in cold and draughty climes. After living in the French Riviera for a while, and taking part in a canoe voyage to Belgium (where at various points he was arrested in the mistaken belief he was a vagrant), he branched out into travel writing, penning *An Inland Voyage* about the canoe trip. He then moved to America, got married and a few years later, aged 38, chartered a yacht to take himself and his wife on an audacious journey to the South Pacific.

For three years, Stevenson travelled between Hawaii, Tahiti, New Zealand and Australia before arriving in Samoa. Liking the look of the island, he bought a parcel of land from a kindly chief and then set about building a grand house in which to live. Due to his intelligence and clever wit, Robert Louis Stevenson became something of a celebrity to the locals, who often sought his counsel on troubling matters. If someone needed advice about whether they had the right to fish along a particular stretch of river or whether they were allowed to plant yams in a certain patch of land, then Stevenson was the man to ask.

In between helping out the locals, he also got involved in the political landscape of Apia which at the time was in the hands of the Germans, British and Americans. He was particularly scathing of the way they were governing the islands. Things got so tense that, at one point, the British almost deported Stevenson back to Scotland. But he managed to cling onto his tropical home and write some more books.

Sadly, in December 1894 aged 44, his poor health caught up with him. As Robert Louis Stevenson was straining to open a bottle of wine, he suffered a massive brain haemorrhage and died. He had lived in Samoa for the final four years of his life. His wife returned to California where she died twenty years later. Their daughter arranged for her body to be transported back to Samoa so she could be buried next to her husband.

I finished my McMuffin and decided I had to see Robert Louis Stevenson's house. It was now a museum called Villa Vailima.

8

I didn't fancy the hour-long trek up the hills to get to Robert Louis Stevenson's former residence, especially in the burgeoning heat of a tropical day in the South Pacific; instead, I asked the hotel to order a taxi for me. The driver was a young man who looked like he knew his way around a rugby pitch.

Rugby is big business in Samoa. First introduced in the 1920s, Samoans took to rugby as Tongans took to mutton flaps. Their first international game was against Fiji, held at 7 am so that the Samoan players could go to work afterwards. They lost 6-0. Since then, they have elevated themselves to the sixteenth best rugby union nation in the world. With a population of around 200,000, about a tenth of them are officially registered as rugby union players.

"Do you play rugby?" I asked the driver as we drove past the clock tower. Overhead, an almost clear blue sky told me it was bloody hot outside.

"Sometimes."

"Are you registered?"

"Yeah, of course." The driver seemed a little annoyed by the question. "All taxi drivers have to be registered."

"No, I meant are you a registered rugby player."

"Oh, I see. No. I just play for fun."

Neither of us said anything for a while and I contented myself by staring out of the window as we threaded through Apia. A pizzeria and a juice bar passed on one side, a petrol station and the Liquor Planet store on the other. Then the gradient shifted and we headed uphill towards the centre of the island. On the plateau was where the rich of Apia lived. Large bungalows featured swings and slides in their expansive grounds. The homes offered residents a lovely view of the city and ocean below. Then the outskirts were gone and we were in the realm of leafy palm trees that swished aside to reveal the occasional village. One of these villages was Vailima where, in January 1890, Robert Louis Stevenson purchased some land.

We turned off the road and arrived at the gatehouse to his old house. It was where to buy tickets. No one was in the booth. The driver shook his head. "Sorry; it must be closed."

I considered this. It seemed we had two choices: depart and go somewhere else or, because there was no barrier stopping us, we would drive into the grounds and see the house from the outside. When I put this second option to the driver, he nodded and we moved forward, driving along a grassy track edged by marker stones. And there it was: the grand residence itself. It looked utterly magnificent; exactly the type of tropical dwelling a famous Nineteenth-century author ought to have resided within.

For a start, it was huge, more of a palace than a house; it reminded me of the Royal Palace in Tonga. The main thrust of the design was a white wooden main section topped with a red-tiled roof, but what set it apart from other buildings in Tonga were the copious drippings of balconies, verandas and colonnades, all set inside a garden of lovely flowers and freshly-cut grass. I jumped out of the car and took a photo just as an elderly blue-shirted gent appeared from the side of the villa. He watched me a while and then turned around the corner again, out of sight.

In 1892, someone had taken a photograph of Robert Louis Stevenson and his wife, plus a few other family members, standing or sitting around the entrance of Villa Vailima. Straw thatch can be seen above their heads which is no longer there. In the old photo, Stevenson is sitting on the steps, looking dapper in a loose shirt and long leather boots. On his head sits a wide-brimmed hat. His expression seems dour, perhaps indicating he was in pain, which he may well have been: two years later he was dead.

I tried to find the place that the photographer had stood upon and, when I thought I had found it, I took another photo, this time of the empty steps.

"You need to pay," said a voice.

I turned to see the blue-shirted man. Evidently, he was a master at creeping up on people. "Pay? I thought the museum was closed?"

"It is, but you need to pay to take photos."

"I haven't taken any." It was a blatant lie but the man was old, and perhaps his eyesight wasn't what it once was.

"I saw you taking them. And there's a camera in your hand."

He had me there. And so I paid the man, haggling him down from the full museum entry fee to just a few tala. He wandered off to resume his lurking and I returned to the car. As we departed via the gatehouse, a woman suddenly appeared. She came to my side door and addressed me. She told me I had to pay the entrance fee that I had failed to settle on the way in.

"You weren't there so I thought it was closed," I said.

"I was visiting the bathroom."

I sighed; the Robert Louis Stevenson museum was turning into a shakedown. But I wasn't about to pay for something when all I had done was take a couple of photos. Besides, I'd already paid. I told the woman about handing over some cash to the old guy.

"What old guy?"

"The guy who works up there. He made me pay for taking some photos."

"There's no guy up there. It's only me."

And so I paid another few tala to get out of the damned place, wondering whether I had met the ghost of the great man himself. If so, he was darker skinned than his photos suggested, but he could be bought off cheaply.

9

The next day, I was wandering around the town again. I walked past the clock tower, the big bank building and then stopped at the best church I had seen on my trip so far: a big blue one that towered over downtown Apia. It was the Immaculate Conception Cathedral, built in 1852 to withstand hurricanes, skirmishes between European colonialists and a disease-ridden congregation.

As the First World War ended, influenza began to rage around the globe, quickly infecting 500 million people. Half a million died in America and a quarter of a million died in England. By the time it reached New Zealand, the world was terrified, and some countries, especially remote island nations, began blockading their ports. But on the 7th November 1918, a cargo ship that had left Auckland arrived in Apia harbour full of sick passengers nursing bleeding noses and terrible sneezes. Instead of being quarantined, the passengers were allowed to set foot onto Samoan soil, unleashing millions of deadly particles as they coughed and sneezed their way into town. Anyone standing close by was infected.

Influenza tore through Samoa. Within a month, almost the whole island was infected, not helped by the Samoan tradition of gathering around a sick person's bed, and the population's daily get-togethers inside the Immaculate Conception Cathedral. With so many people suffering from influenza, it was inevitable that the death toll would be high. In the end, because of that ship, one on five Samoans died: the highest mortality rate of any country during the two-year epidemic. Across in American Samoa, they prevented the flu arriving by a timely blockade of their ports. Not one person died of influenza there. The deaths in Western Samoa caused lingering resentment of New Zealand for many years to come.

I stared up at the cathedral. Its front facade had been looking out across Apia's waterfront for a century and a half. It had witnessed the arrival of Robert Louis Stevenson's boat and it saw the ridiculous stand-off between German, American and British war boats that ended with most of them sunk. It even watched a boat carrying influenza come into port unhindered with its cargo of disease. But in 2009, the cathedral saw its greatest challenge yet.

One hundred and twenty miles off the coast of Samoa, an 8.1 magnitude rumbled under the Pacific Ocean. As well as shaking the islands, it unleashed a dreadful tsunami which struck Samoa's coastlines with waves taller than a house. In Apia, timely tsunami warnings meant everyone evacuated to higher ground, but in the southern part of the island, home to numerous fishing villages, people didn't have time to leave.

One hotelier on the south coast described how the ocean quickly engulfed her establishment, causing the hotel's back door to fly open with the force of water. Immediately immersed in sea water, she swirled around for a few moments before feeling the water recede. But this was not a gentle withdraw; this was a ferocious liquid retreat. Had she not managed to grab onto a door handle on the way out, she would be dead.

Elsewhere, a father had watched the tidal wave smash through his village. As it came upon him, he desperately clung to his children but, with the water crashing around him, he lost his grip on the youngest, a little boy aged just one. Five hours later, following a frantic search, the father found him on a nearby beach, face down on the sand. Expecting the worst, the distraught man picked him up, shook him a little and was amazed when the boy fluttered his eyelids. He was fine.

Others were not so lucky: twenty villages were destroyed and one hundred people were dead or missing. Three thousand people were rendered homeless by the time the waves had ebbed back from whence they came.

Apia on the northern coast survived the ravages the south took, but the Immaculate Conception Cathedral was damaged. The earthquake rattled it so much that it was deemed unsafe for use. After three years of restoration, its new look was unveiled to a much-admiring public. People nodded and nudged one another. Instead of a simple white design, it now featured blue domes and turrets, finished with stained-glass windows. Against a blue sky, it looked stunning.

Adjoining it was the Immaculate Religious Shop & Café, but I bypassed it in favour of entering the cathedral via the Door of Mercy. As expected, the interior could not live up the exterior but I stolen some items and then set fire to the place. Another case involved a Chinese man who had somehow lost control of his car which had then slammed into a bus. In the resulting fire, a 58-year-old passenger had died. A third court case was about a drinking session which had turned ugly. After boozing the night away, three pals had fallen out and killed one of their party. The most troubling courthouse deliberation, at least for me, concerned a man accused of robbing an American couple walking along the seawall upon which I'd just traipsed. As the tourists sauntered along, enjoying a pleasant Samoan evening, a man had rushed them from behind, grabbed the woman's handbag and pushed her to the ground. He then ran off, with the woman's boyfriend in hot pursuit. With the help of another man who had witnessed this foul play, the American chased the criminal into the ocean, subdued him and then handed over the drenched and spluttering thief to the police.

As I made my way back to the hotel, I kept an eye on people walking the seawall with me, but apart from a trio of teenage girls blasting hip-hop music from some portable speakers, I had the wall to myself. Back outside my hotel, I paused for a moment, regarding the sprawl of Apia. It may not be the prettiest capital city in the world, but it wasn't doing too badly for itself. It had a wonderful church and a great slice of Pacific Ocean, even if the locals were doing their best to fill its edges with litter. Later, as I packed my bags for my flight to Sydney, I came to the conclusion that although Tonga and Samoa were cut from the same piece of tropically-fused cloth, they were both distinct nations in their own right, maybe not as different as Spain is from France, but certainly as different as Spain is from Portugal.

My final stop promised to be vastly different to them both Samoa and Tonga and indeed anywhere else I'd been on my trip. Not a South Pacific nation as such, the lure of East Timor, or Timor-Leste as it is more commonly known, was too much of a pull to say no to on my way home. Besides, East Timor more or less counted because it was in the Pacific. So after a night in Sydney and a couple of nights in Bali with my wife, I would be heading into my final and eighth country.

Top L-R: *Looking towards Apia from the seawall; The colourful buses that ply Apia's island routes*
Middle L-R: *Apia Clock Tower – capable of time travel; The amazing Immaculate Conception Cathedral; Colourful Samoan tala*
Bottom L-R: *A traditional Samoan Meeting House that needs some restoration work; The view from a taxi: gorgeous!*

CHAPTER 8. DILI, EAST TIMOR

Interesting fact: East Timor is one of only two predominantly Christian countries in South East Asia (the other being the Philippines).

Unpleasant thoughts run through my mind as we descend through bad turbulence aboard the EU-banned airliner. These thoughts intensify as the shakes and rattles increase and the cabin crew scurry to their seats for safety. Even the ceaseless chatter – a constant noise that had hummed from taking off until now – subsided and then ended. The beige-robed nuns opposite had stopped talking. The couple by the window next to me stopped talking. Everyone on the plane had stopped talking. The silence inside the cabin was disproportionate to the scream of the jets outside. All my running from Cyclone Keni and now an unknown storm had caught up with me over the skies of East Timor.

The name of the airline did little to instil confidence either. Nam Air brought to mind low-level sorties across Vietnamese jungles, even though the name had nothing to do with Vietnam; its name came from the surname of one of the owners. Even so, with the buffeting continuing and the wing tips undulating like a conductor's baton, my brain concluded it was only a matter of time before a hellacious cracking sound resounded – the signal that doom was upon us with the detachment of a wing.

Outside, there was nothing but water. It was occasionally visible through thick cloud. And then a mass of land appeared: the island of Timor. Then it was gone to the clouds. Another lurch befell our stricken aircraft causing a moment of pure panic. Someone screamed and, inexplicably, someone laughed. And then, as abruptly as we had entered it, we cleared the turbulent air and descended into calm. People looked around the cabin as if they were dreaming. Was that it? Was the plane okay now? It appeared it was.

    The island reappeared, and was more distinct now and getting closer. A chime binged and a gruff voice instructed the cabin crew to be seated for landing. They already were. Then Dili became visible – the low-level capital of East Timor, a city of almost a quarter of a million that straddled the ocean and was backed by brown highlands. After flying parallel to the airport, the flight crew executed a well-performed turn over the ocean to line up with the runway. A few minutes later, we are down in East Timor and the cabin chatter resumed as if nothing had happened. Nam Air 280 pulled off the jungle-flanked runway to trundle to the small terminal. It was time to begin my final adventure.

2

I was the second passenger to deplane, walking behind the solitary passenger who had paid for a business class seat: a forty-something Chinese man who, for no fathomable reason, was now walking slower than a sloth towards the terminal building. With a horde on my tail, I decided to break business class protocol and overtake the slowcoach so I could reach immigration first. As I began to pass the man from China, I was momentarily flummoxed when he decided to speed up. The game was on.

    Because we were walking along a narrow open-air corridor, he easily gained the upper hand, especially with his hand luggage dragging behind him. I breathed on his neck, but he didn't give an inch, and then, when he realised he could walk on the left but pull his luggage on the right, he knew he could slow down. I seethed, huffed and puffed but the presence of men in uniforms and with guns put me off felling him with a leg swipe. Instead, I followed hot on his tail until we came to a turn. In front was a booth that said Visa on Arrival. To the right was a sign which said Immigration and

Baggage Retrieval. The man from China slowed and assessed the choices. Inwardly, I smiled. He was surely in need of a visa and, indeed, that's what he plumbed for. In victory, I sidestepped his luggage and bounded towards immigration.

"Stop!" commanded a man in uniform. He was standing at the point of the turn. Behind me, the horde was fast approaching and would be upon me any second. "Where are you from?"

"England," I said with short breath.

"You mean the United Kingdom?"

I nodded, itching to be on the move.

"You need a visa." He pointed to where the man from China was. A passenger bypassed me to the right.

I shook my head. "No visa."

The guard didn't say anything and watched a couple more passengers slip by. He didn't say anything to them but, then again, they looked like locals. Finally, he glanced my way. "Go there. You must get a visa. Look." He unfolded a piece of paper from his pocket and showed it to me. It contained a long list of countries together with a tick or a cross signifying whether a citizen of that country needed a visa. As far as I could tell, only three countries had ticks: China, Ireland and the United Kingdom. Mentally crying and almost wishing we had crashed into the sea, I gave up my immigration pole position and traipsed to the Visa on Arrival booth, taking my place, once again, behind the man from China. He soon finished and wandered off. I moved forward and, ten minutes and thirty dollars later, I followed him to join the back of the immigration line.

Out in the sunshine, the scene was chaotic. People were blocking the terminal waiting for arriving relatives. Taxi drivers were shouting for customers and even the East Timor football team was in attendance. Whether they were waiting to be picked up or about to fly I had no clue because arrivals and departures were in the same place.

I brushed off three taxi drivers in quick succession and searched for a man with a sign. My name would be written on it, the hotel had assured me via an email. Well, they were wrong because no one had a sign with my name or anybody else's name for that matter. Sighing, I stepped into the shade and watched the football team instead. The whole group was posing near a counter, while an older man, presumably their manager, lined up his camera. Everyone watched while he did this, even the taxi drivers and, when the manager had finished, his team cheered, which brought about a round of applause from the audience. It was at this point that I noticed the man from China again. He was standing a short distance away, scouring the chaos. I watched him check a printed piece of paper and then shake his head in annoyance. It looked like he'd been left out in the heat, too.

Fifteen minutes later, the crowd thinned as my fellow passengers went on their way and the arriving passengers dispersed. The football team went inside and so this left about eight taxi drivers, a woman selling wooden crocodiles, plus me and the man from China. So from first place, we had been relegated to last.

The same taxi driver who had approached me twice already came over once more. He didn't say anything, just waited for my latest response. But before I could answer, the man from China came over, too. "You speak English?" he asked in a thick accent.

I nodded.

"You wait for hotel to pick up?"

I nodded again.

"Hotel Timor?"

"Yes."

The man from China nodded miserably. "Same hotel as me. I do not think they come. I think we share a taxi, yes?"

I nodded for the third time. The waiting taxi driver had heard the word taxi and looked very interested. After establishing that the fare would be a fixed at ten dollars (East Timor uses the US dollar as its currency), we followed him to the car. The Chinese man was now my best friend in East Timor.

Dili looked fairly sprightly from inside a car, with a few modern developments mixed around older buildings. The commercial zone was made up of snack shacks, motorbike repair shops and stalls selling flip-flops. With almost the whole population Catholic, there were a few churches in the mix, too.

The man from China introduced himself as Yichu. He was a structural engineer on a short posting to Dili to oversee construction of a new building project in the capital. It was his third such posting and he was not a fan of the country. "There is nothing to do. Each day is same: work, work, hotel, sleep."

For me, as a first time visitor, things were more exciting. After all, I was in a brand new country and what was better than that?

3

East Timor occupies the eastern half of Timor Island and is the poorest country in South East Asia. For thousands of years, the inhabitants of Timor grew crops, procured wax and honey from the island's massive bee population and generally lived a peaceful life. They were also good fishermen, able to catch fish in deeper parts of the ocean than anyone had done before them. Occasionally, Chinese traders would arrive on the island to barter rice and textiles but, by and large, the people were left alone to get on with their lives. This all changed when the Portuguese arrived in the Sixteenth century.

At first, it was just a few monks who turned up, converting some people to Catholicism, but, after poking around in the jungle for a while, some of them discovered sizeable quantities of sandalwood which they brought to the attention of passing Portuguese traders. So valuable was sandalwood that when news of its discovery reached Europe, the Portuguese sent ships full of settlers to set up a small trading outpost in Eastern Timor. That done, the Europeans planted a flag on a hill and declared that the eastern portion of Timor was now a Portuguese colony. Over on the western side of the island, the

Dutch set up their own colony and between them, they drew up a border which split the island in half.

For 150 years, the Portuguese bled their colony dry. Then World War II broke out and the Japanese came to take over. In the resulting Battle of Timor, tens of thousands of local men and women died trying to fend them off. But it was all in vain; Japan won and East Timor was under Japanese occupation for the duration of the war. The Portuguese returned following Japan's surrender and continued where they had left off, extracting as many natural resources as they could until 1975 when they packed up and left. East Timor was finally independent of European rule, just like West Timor had been since 1945 when the Dutch had handed their colony over to Indonesia.

For nine days, East Timor was in charge of its affairs. Then Indonesian troops stormed in, all guns blazing. They were backed by Australia and the United States who offered funding and, more importantly, legitimacy for the invasion. For Australia, Indonesia was a favoured trading partner and it did not want to sully this relationship. The Americans were worried about Communists taking over East Timor, as they had in Vietnam, and so thought it better to have Indonesia, a known quantity, in control rather than allow the locals to make a mess of it. So the people of East Timor didn't stand a chance and, in the blink of an eye, they swapped one foreign power for another. The Indonesian rulers were far harsher than the Portuguese and, for the next quarter of a century, they repressed the people of East Timor in horrendous ways. But outside of this little slice of East Asia, no one knew what was going on because the Indonesian government kept a lid on things. That all changed in 1991.

Renewed calls for independence caught the ears of Portugal. Still feeling guilty about the way they had abandoned its former colony, the Portuguese government decided to send a delegation to East Timor to look at what was going on. A few journalists caught wind of this and decided to go too. However, the Indonesian government objected to Portuguese involvement and told them to back off. Quivering in their European boots, the Portuguese did exactly that and called the whole thing off. No one bothered to tell the journalists, though, and they arrived in Dili.

With tensions running high in the capital due to the Portuguese pull-out, Indonesian troops took a gamble and shot dead one of the independence movement's key supporters, an eighteen-year-old man called Sebastiao Gomes. They hoped that this quick show of force would quell other activists from starting trouble. And their ploy worked because, for the next two weeks, Dili was calm.

Then the funeral of Gomes was held. Because it was deemed sufficiently newsworthy, the foreign journalists who had remained in Dili decided to attend his memorial service. While they set up their cameras in the Santa Cruz Cemetery, thousands of independence protesters were taking to the streets of Dili, shouting and waving banners, hoping their dispute would make it onto foreign news channels. Indonesian troops watched the funeral procession with keen interest but kept their weapons under control. Despite the noise and bluster, things were peaceful.

Until, suddenly, they weren't.

After standing idle for so long, Indonesian soldiers began to beat protesters. It was as if they had been given the all-clear to wade in hard. When some protesters fought back, they were shot or stabbed to death. However, this was a sideline to the main event. As the main thrust of protesters reached the Santa Cruz Cemetery, Indonesian troops and police closed in and surrounded them. Then they opened fire with machine guns. Mourners scrambled for cover behind gravestones, some managing to evade bullets, some not. A couple of American journalists selflessly acted as human shields to stop some of the soldiers firing at protestors. For this, they received harsh beatings – one ending up with a fractured skull. People everywhere were being shot, stabbed or bayoneted by Indonesian troops. By the time the killing stopped, 250 unarmed civilians lay dead. But unbeknown to the Indonesians, a British reporter had secretly filmed the attack.

Somehow his video footage was smuggled out of East Timor where it was broadcast on British TV. Outrage was immediate and, even though Indonesia tried to play the killings down by claiming the event had been a 'misunderstanding', it was devastating for them. Foreign aid ceased and the Portuguese government finally stepped in to help the people of East Timor. A referendum was held in 1998 and the people of East Timor defiantly said they wanted independence. In response, Indonesia tore down electricity pylons, generators, schools and water systems: infrastructure they had built and paid for. The UN sent thousands of peacekeeping troops to restore order and to save what was left. By May 2002, Indonesian troops had gone and East Timor was an independent nation. It was the newest country on the planet until South Sudan gained its independence in 2011.

4

After checking into the Timor Hotel (and receiving abounding apologies for the lack of an airport pick up, plus $5 each for the taxi we had paid), Yichu and I went our separate ways. He went straight to the hotel bar while I regarded the huge 4x4 car in the lobby. Often seen in plush shopping malls, I'd never seen a show car in a hotel before. The only people who could afford such vehicles in East Timor were foreigners, I guessed, and so what better way to show it off than have it gleaming in the middle of the best hotel in the city.

Two middle-aged Australian men walked past me, heading through the doors onto the street. Australians make up a fair percentage of foreign ex-pats in East Timor. The country's healthy offshore oil deposits (50% of its revenue comes from petrochemicals), attract them even though the oil and gas fields are a source of contention between both nations. When East Timor became independent in 2002, the maritime boundary that separated it from Australia was blurred. So amid the confusion, both sides laid claim to fields worth billions of dollars. Strained negotiations are still ongoing.

After dropping off my things in the room, I left the hotel and assessed the state of my immediate surroundings. The road in front of the hotel was called Avenue Almirante Americo Tomas, named after a former Portuguese president. It was busy but not overly so. I was surprised to see a Burger King restaurant just down the road. Trucks and mopeds rolled past, as did mikrolets: vans converted into passenger carriers. Like the buses of Samoa, most of them featured wacky designs and bright colour schemes and were always full of locals. Old yellow taxis patrolled at slower speeds, beeping whenever they saw me.

On the other side of the road was the port. Large shipping containers stacked like giant blocks of Lego blocked any view of the ocean, and so I set off in search of it; first stopping at a small but busy park called Garden 5th May, the date of East Timor's independence referendum. People were sitting on benches reading paperbacks or chatting as they ambled through. Plenty of young couples were sitting around, too, some with arms curled around each other or else holding hands. No one paid me the slightest bit of attention as I strolled to a large and dramatic statue in the middle. The figure at the top of the plinth was a bare-chested warrior breaking free of the chains of Indonesian oppression.

Following independence from Indonesia, things did not run smoothly for the fledgeling nation. Four years in, violence broke out across East Timor, mainly due to high unemployment. Buildings in Dili were damaged, cars set alight and shops looted. Then full-scale rioting began and people either escaped the city or sought safety in refugee camps, such as the one set up in Garden 5th May. With the country on the brink of civil war, The UN stepped in and restored order again. They stayed for the next six years. Since 2012, East Timor has been peaceful. But it is an edgy peace.

5

It was hot, that much was obvious. But with the sun shining and a blue sky, I was in a buoyant mood as I left the park, walking along a coastal road past the port. Once past the shipping containers, the Pacific Ocean appeared: a beautiful blue dotted with ships and large rugged islands in the distance. I kept a keen eye out for saltwater crocodiles because some had recently been seen in Dili.

I found a seafront park that was either under construction or else dilapidated. Exposed pipes lay across its surface, and half-finished pathways had crumbled into the soil and grass. Even so, plenty of young East Timorese couples were sitting on the seawall, keeping to the shade under the palms. Snapping reptiles were not pursuing them and thus I concluded it was safe. I walked over to the seawall; peering over the edge, ready to spring back should I see anything untoward; all I could see was a lapping ocean and a man standing in the surf with a fishing net. If anyone was going to be taken by a crocodile, it was him.

I meandered across another broken path towards a statue in the middle of the park. It was huge. The giants on it were men, one dead or dying and the other supporting his prone body. The man cradling was fashioned with a face of pure anguish. Looking at it was painful.

Even though it didn't say, the monument was in remembrance to the people who had perished in the Santa Cruz massacre. Sebastiao Gomes, the man whose death had kick-started the massacre, was shot nearby – just over the road. Before Indonesian soldiers killed him, they had pulled Gomes out of the church opposite where I stood: the oldest Catholic place of worship in the country. I left the statue and walked over to it, finding that the Motael Church's best feature was its weather vane. Instead of a cockerel or a compass arrow, it featured a sailing ship. And though I walked around the church and through its grounds, I could find no evidence of the horror that had occurred almost three decades previously. But perhaps that was a good thing.

Because I was a fair distance away from Dili's town centre, the streets were nearly silent; almost devoid of moving vehicles. Only occasionally did a motorbike pass me. I walked past a couple of small, shack-like cafes with plastic chairs outside for non-existent patrons. A couple of teenage boys were hanging around the entrance of one shack, doing nothing in particular, not even looking at me. I carried on until I arrived on the main street where the traffic was busier. My immediate goal was the Presidential Palace, a ten-minute walk away, but something else took my attention: a man sitting on the pavement. He was doing something I'd never witnessed before.

He was aged about thirty, wiry thin, and was sitting outside the locked doors of a convenience store. On his lap was a white Styrofoam box piled with yellow rice, chunks of meat and some hideous-looking brown sauce. The man was not eating it; he was rubbing the meal into his scalp. As I passed, I could see greasy globules mixed into his hair and fingers. After sidestepping him (where I was sure he wasn't even aware of me passing), I could not think of a single reasonable reason with which to explain his actions. So perturbed, I stopped and turned back. The man was still rubbing his meal into his head with thick, horrible handfuls of meat and rice shampoo.

6

The Presidential Palace was the finest building in town. For a start, it was huge and modern and it commanded a wide space inside well-manicured gardens. It was far back enough from the road to avoid the shakes and rumbles of passing traffic, but close enough to it should the president want to get out and drive somewhere.

I peered through the metal fence. The palace was a wide rectangular block of white with a dark central section that featured grand steps, a plethora of flagpoles and a pair of traditionally-dressed guards draped in skirts with pineapples on their heads. Upon closer inspection, I saw the headwear was not fruit based but long, fluffy rooster feathers. Both men looked supremely bored, one of them even eyeing himself in a handheld mirror while he squeezed a spot. Then one of them noticed me and waved me away. I took that as my cue to leave and headed back along the highway.

Dili seemed perfectly safe, I realised. The pavements were in a good state; same with the roads. The people seemed a placid bunch, too, a few smiling as I passed. Even so, I was still thinking of the advice given by the UK Foreign Office, who warned that if I saw any groups of young men who looked like they were part of a martial arts group, then I might want to run in the other direction.

Since independence, gangs of karate, judo, taekwondo and pencak silat (an Indonesian martial art) aficionados have been responsible for a lot of petty crime in the city, sometimes even offering their services out as mobs for hire. Martial art turf wars used to grow so heated that on some occasions people were killed. In 2013, these gangs were so prevalent on Dili's streets that the government banned all martial arts and closed down schools that taught it. The pastime went underground but occasionally came up for air and the UK government wanted visitors to Dili to keep well clear of it did. I swept my eyes to the left and then to the right, bounding forward with a headlong kick.

I found myself near the hotel again, and this time headed in the other direction. A yellow taxi crept alongside and beeped, the driver looking hopeful, but I waved him away with a kung fu jab. I followed the course of a road that led me past a woman with a pole straddling her shoulders. Dangling from each end were small buckets filled with water bottles for sale. I bought one for a dollar and continued on my way.

After turning right, passing a florist that specialised in funeral bouquets, I walked close to the national football stadium of East Timor, a place where controversy once reigned supreme. As part of their efforts to secure a place in the 2023 Asian Cup games, the East Timor football management did something spectacularly devious. When it became apparent that their players were not cutting the mustard, the management team went rogue and secretly sent some trusted scouts to Brazil. After scouring small time football clubs, the scouts found a dozen Brazilian players in possession of skills greater than any home-grown talent. After buttering them up about how good they were, the scouts took them somewhere quiet and asked whether they wanted to play for the East Timor national team. When the Brazilians pointed out that people from their country were not allowed to play for other international teams, the agents shushed them and told them of their dastardly plan. Each footballer would receive a forged birth certificate, a false passport (claiming they were citizens of East Timor) and a briefcase stuffed with cash. With the strange deal struck, the Brazilians were flown to Dili and sent into secret training. After a suitable time, the management of the East Timor football team announced that they had found some 'newly discovered talent'. As soon as the new players were incorporated into the national team, East Timor began to win qualifying matches. Things were looking good until FIFA somehow discovered the subterfuge. The upshot was that East Timor was banned from the competition, the Brazilians sent home, and the name of East Timor sullied among the football world.

Not far from the stadium of shame was perhaps the grandest monument in Dili: a circular parade of reds, blacks and yellows. The colours belonged to an array of East Timor flags surrounding the statue of a tall, suited man holding one finger aloft. It was Francisco Xavier do Amaral, who, in 1975, briefly became the nation's first president until Indonesian troops rolled in nine days later. The Indonesians exiled Amaral to Bali, forcing him to work as a servant in the household of General Kalbuadi, the leader of the East Timor invasion force. When East Timor gained independence in 2002, Amaral returned to the country of his birth and ran for president. Unfortunately, he failed and he died in 2012, which is a shame as it would have made for a happy ending to the story. Still, he had a good statue.

7

Back in my hotel room after some lunch, I had an altercation with a lizard. It started innocently enough with me noticing the thin reptile sitting on the floor outside of the bathroom door. It was utterly still, its head pointing upward; an immensely long tail curling across the carpet. From head to tail, it was about ten inches long. Thinking it was perhaps dead, or dulled into inaction by the cold air conditioning; I bent down and prodded its tail. It didn't move a muscle, not even its eyes. I could tell it was alive though, due to the slight breathing movement in its chest.

I hate it whenever I come across an animal in distress, and thinking that this lizard needed to be in the warmth, I decided to pick it up. I could take it outside where the sun would warm it sufficiently so it could get on with its day. As I carefully reached for the soft area just behind its front legs, it came alive and let rip. Thinking I was a predator, it twisted its neck and sunk its gnashers into the side of my thumb. The pain was immediate as if someone had suddenly clamped a strong bulldog clip onto my digit. In localised agony, I was suddenly at a loss what to do. My mercy mission had turned into a lizard attack and the reptile was now dangling from my hand, teeth firmly shut against my skin.

In desperation, I rushed over to the window and somehow opened it with my free hand. A ledge where the lizard could escape was within reaching distance and so I dangled my hand enticingly over it, hoping it would let go and flee. It didn't, it remained clamped to my throbbing thumb and I wondered whether it was sucking my blood. Just as I was about to reach panic stations, it must have realised it had an escape option because it released its jaws, dropped to the ledge and scuttled away, disappearing from view. At the same time, I was staring at my thumb, amazed to see it was not bleeding. There were no teeth marks at all, just a red D-shaped indentation on the side. After that excitement, I decided it was time to go and see a massive statue of Jesus Christ.

The taxi driver, whose name I never caught, was a thin, fifty-something, gent who drove a taxi with the creakiest suspension I'd heard in a long while. It groaned and squeaked even while stationary. Surprisingly, he could speak excellent English. "I used to drive UN workers around," he told me by way of an explanation of his linguistic skills. "From 1999 to 2013, I drove them all around East Timor and I learned English then. So why are you here in Dili? Work?"

I told him I was a tourist. We were driving along the main highway near the port, heading eastward.

The man's eyes widened. "Tourist!" He shook his head and laughed.

"I take it you don't get many here, then?"

"Put it this way, you're the first tourist I've ever had in this taxi. Some of my friends have driven young Australian backpackers around, but never someone from Europe. I can't wait to tell them. When we stop, I might take a photo of you, if that's alright. So what do you think?"

"That's fine."

"No, I meant what do you think of Dili?"

I looked outside. We were passing the ocean again, another tropical slice of Pacific that had been my ever-present companion throughout the trip. "It's safe and clean, and the people seem friendly. It's expensive though."

The driver nodded. "Very expensive. Like these houses here." They were on our right-hand side, most with barbed wire protection and 4x4s parked in their drives. "This is where the rich people live – foreign workers, mostly; maybe a few locals. The rent is two, maybe three thousand dollars."

I whistled appropriately, even though three thousand dollars didn't seem overly extortionate to me. Spread over a year, it worked out at two hundred and fifty dollars a month, about £170. Not bad for a large house with an ocean view.

The driver said, "That's thirty-six thousand dollars a year."

I shot him a glance. "So it's three thousand dollars per month?"

"Yeah, a month. What did you think . . . a year?" He laughed.

We drove on for a few minutes and then caught up with a large, open-backed 4x4 with five teenage girls sitting in the back. The girls were enjoying themselves as their hair whipped around their heads. Then the road opened into an area of mangrove which, the taxi driver said, was a popular haunt of crocodiles. I asked whether he'd ever seen one.

"Only once," he told me. "A very big one. I was on my bike and I saw it moving in the mangroves. When I stopped it disappeared under the water and I pedalled away quicker than I've ever pedalled before. But this was many years ago when I was a teenager."

"But they're still here?"

"Yeah. Sometimes they eat fishermen."

Ahead of us was a curve of delicious coastline set against a backdrop of hills. It reminded me of somewhere in the Middle East, perhaps Oman. With a clear road, we managed to overtake the 4x4, the girls waving as we passed, and sped along for a few minutes until we rounded a bend and saw it: the statue of Christ, standing, like a poor man's version of Rio's Christ the Redeemer, on a high hilltop ledge.

"How many steps to get to the top?" I asked the driver as we closed in on Dili's number one tourist attraction.

"Five hundred."

A walk in the park, then.

8

Twenty years into their occupation, the Indonesian government offered their East Timor province a gift: a 90-foot copper statue of Jesus Christ which they placed high up on a hill in Dili. It was a gesture of goodwill aimed at appeasing local dissent, and a bold one: a Christian symbol from a Muslim nation could have easily gone the wrong way. But it seemed to do the trick, at least for a little while.

As well as the statue, Indonesian engineers built a chapel that they embedded into the rock underneath. It was a place to pray before attempting to climb the steps. On my way to begin the trek, I glanced into the dark chapel, tipped my hat and then set forth on the ascent.

At first, it was okay, but then, for the remaining 499 steps, I fought an inner demon which wanted me to stop after every ten or so steps. At the rate I was going, it would take two hours to reach the summit, which was ridiculous. Not helping matters were the people climbing with me or coming down the other way. Everybody in Dili was out in force to see Christ, it seemed. And then there were the joggers: keep-fit maniacs in Lycra who were running up the bloody thing. Whenever they reached one of the resting points, they would jog on the spot for a minute before carrying on upward. I wondered whether to karate chop the next one who came past.

I wheezed upwards, sweating and panting; occasionally stopping to slurp mouthfuls of water. And then, perhaps miraculously, I made it to the uppermost viewing platform. High above me, standing on a giant globe, was the Lord. At times like these, a Tongan church choir ought to be on hand to add a suitable soundtrack.

Jesus was in better shape than the globe, pulling a classic pose of Lordly calm with arms spread wide as if welcoming travellers from afar. Beneath his feet, Planet Earth was stained orange from residue leaching from its copper continents. If taken to scale, each landmass had dirty orange-green sediment reaching across its ocean for hundreds of miles.

While I waited for my pulse to slow, I got chatting to a man who was up there with his wife and young daughter. After finding out I was British and that I was a tourist, he was eager to know what I thought of his country.

"It's great. Everyone I've met has been super friendly. And this statue is good. And so is the view." I gestured to the expanse of ocean and the green-topped hills. His wife and daughter both looked to where I was pointing and then resumed their vigil of my face.

The man nodded thoughtfully. "I wish more tourists would come here, but I don't think they will."

"Why not?"

"For one thing, it is hard to get here. The only direct flights are from Darwin and Bali, and sometimes Singapore. And we don't have much in the way of tourist infrastructure here. But I think the main reason people don't come here is they believe Timor-Leste is dangerous, a legacy from when UN peacekeepers were here. But you did not think this or you would not have come. Is this true?"

I concurred with his assessment, not really knowing what to say. "I've found it completely safe."

"As would everyone else who came. But it will take many years, perhaps decades for them to come." He held out his hand and I shook it, feeling a lit bit embarrassed. He said, "I want to thank you for visiting my country, especially since you came all the way from the United Kingdom."

"Thanks for having me," I answered, rather limply. I smiled at the woman and the little girl and then headed for the steps.

9

At the bottom of the steps, I found the taxi driver waiting at our prearranged rendezvous point in the car park, and we were soon on our way back to Dili. He was going to show me a lighthouse before dropping me off at the city's best shopping mall.

"So what's life like here?" I asked.

"It's good," he said jovially. "I have a job and own my own house. My wife is happy and my children are happy. The government could be better. But I think everyone says this, no matter which country they live in."

"What about the police? Are they okay?"

He gave a slight pause. "So-so."

I got the impression he did not want to talk about that aspect of life in East Timor.

The taxi slowed because there was a huddle of people on our side of the road crowding around a mobile food stall. A small boy was receiving a walloping from his mother for straying too far into the road. Next to him, a couple of scrawny chickens pecked in the undergrowth. The taxi driver said, "We love eating chicken in East Timor. But do you know where they come from?"

I gestured to the chickens by the side of the road.

The driver shook his head. "No, not those. They are Timor chickens; too expensive for most people. Most of our chickens come from Brazil. Can you believe that? Chickens all the way from Brazil." He began to chuckle in a manner not dissimilar to a squawking hen. I didn't know what to say to that so said nothing, just taking in the sights and sounds of Dili as we neared the central core again: a wedding celebration in a large marquee; some raucous reggae music blasting out from a bar; a family of five squeezed onto a single moped; a pile of burning rubbish by the side of the road and a stall selling coconuts and bananas. Dili was awash with colour and activity.

The Farol Lighthouse was a bit of a let-down. Instead of a tall cone-shaped lighthouse, it had a stripy white and green base, and a main section supported on thin scaffolding. It was the second most disappointing lighthouse I'd seen on my trip. Even so, the lighthouse had attracted quite a crowd of locals, a few of whom were sitting on its outer fence facing the sea. The rest were doing various forms of keep-fit. One man, utterly unabashed by his actions, was hopping like a frog. He looked ridiculous, but no one else seemed bothered. Another man was stretching from side to side like a mad contortionist.

10

In most cities, Timor Plaza wouldn't be anything special. Yes, it had a Gloria Jean's Coffee, a gym and a cinema, but it was a generic – and on the small side – shopping mall. The friendly taxi driver deposited me outside the main entrance and suggested I head up to the Sky Bar to have a drink and enjoy a panoramic view of Dili. I thanked him for his service and said farewell.

To get to the elevator, I had to walk past a collection of clothes, shoe and cosmetic stores, similar to others in any mall across the world. The only difference was the price. Dili was more expensive than many European capitals.

As I stepped into the empty lift, three women in their thirties rushed inside. None acknowledged me, resuming their non-stop conversation about nothing in particular – the hairdresser, an altercation one of them had with a taxi driver and a long complaint about their child's rude teacher. All three were Australian and when the lift pinged open on the fifth floor, I realised they were heading to the Sky Bar, too. Through a set of doors, we walked, under the scrutiny of a security guard. Then we entered an open-roofed terrace with a bar at one end and a restaurant at the other. There were five or six other people already there, all of them Westerners apart from a Chinese man sitting by himself.

I wondered where to go. The Australian women were veterans and headed straight for the restaurant with a swirl of perfume and heels. They joined a table with two other women. I opted for the bar, wondering whether I should sit down or order a drink first. The problem was solved when a waitress approached. She looked at me expectantly.

"A beer please," I said.

"Tiger, Heineken or Bintang?"

I didn't want Singaporean, German or Indonesian beer; I always preferred to try to the local stuff. "Does East Timor have its own beer?"

The waitress looked at me in confusion "Yes, we have our own beer: Tiger, Heineken or Bintang."

I thought it pointless explaining that I wanted a beer brewed in East Timor as opposed a beer sold in East Timor. I opted for a Tiger Beer from Singapore. The woman nodded and waited. I repeated that

I wanted a Tiger Beer and again she nodded and waited. After a few seconds of awkward silence, she told me that I needed to pay four dollars first.

I handed over some cash and when the bottle came I relocated to the edge of the terrace so I could see Dili from above. The view wasn't that great, mainly the mall's car park, a few nondescript buildings and some trees. It was underwhelming actually and so I decided to sit in the restaurant and order a pizza.

As I waited for my food, the bar gradually filled up. Every patron, apart from a huddle of Chinese men who had joined the man from earlier, was Western and, had it not been for the tropical weather and local bar staff, I could have been in Europe. Still, my pizza was nice, far better than the atrocity I'd had in the Solomon Islands. And then my Chinese pal turned up. He had been heading towards the Chinese group when he noticed me.

"Come and sit with us," he said. "You should not be sitting alone."

I almost took him up on his offer, but I had already finished my beer and pizza and wanted to get back to the hotel. I was dog-tired after so much walking over the last few weeks. "I think I'm just going to head back to the hotel. I've got to pack for my flight tomorrow. Thanks for the offer, though."

"Leaving so soon? You are the lucky one."

11

So that was it, another trip complete: eight countries, all of them with coastlines on the mighty Pacific Ocean. From the raskols of Port Moresby to the squeaky cleanliness (and eye-watering expensiveness) of Auckland; from the beaches of Fiji to the sleepiness of Tonga, I'd seen an awful lot. True, I had not lingered long in each place, which seemed almost criminal considering the distances travelled to get to some of these places, but I felt I had gained a sense of what each city offered. Of course, with more time,

I might have visited the island in Vanuatu where bungee jumping was invented or the rainforest reserve in Samoa where it is possible to climb into the canopy to sleep in a tree house. I might have taken a boat trip to Vava'u in Tonga, where, if I timed it right, I could observe humpback whales up close. But alas, those things would have to wait for another time.

But which country was my favourite? That was the question my wife asked when I met up with her in Bali the next afternoon. And as strange as it was, I thought it might be Papua New Guinea. Often, I find that the countries I had the lowest expectations for ended up being the best. I had been dreading Port Moresby; yet, I'd found it an exciting, vibrant city full of friendly people and interesting sights. The memory of being in the company of a Papua New Guinean chieftain armed with a machete would stay with me forever, as would the drive I took along a street in prime raskol territory. But as well as Papua New Guinea, I'd also enjoyed watching the fishing pigs in Tonga, seeing Robert Louis Stevenson's house in Samoa and sampling kava in Fiji. The South Pacific region may be difficult to get to, but for those who manage it, the rewards are high.

Top L-R: *East Timor Parliament Building; I Love Dili!; Statue in Garden 5th May symbolising breaking free the shackles of Indonesian rule*
Middle L-R: *Santa Cruz Massacre Monument – bigger than it looks; The Statue of Christ on a tall hill; Motael Church, where Indonesian troops killed an activist*
Bottom L-R: *East Timor Flag; Statue of Francisco Xavier do Amaral, East Timor's first president*

Message from Jason

Thanks for reading about my travels around the South Pacific and beyond. If you enjoyed it, I would really appreciate a review on Amazon. Just a few lines will do. Small-time authors such as me rely on word-of-mouth exposure. Just head over to Amazon, search 'Jason Smart' and leave a review.

If you have enjoyed reading this book by Jason Smart, then perhaps you will also enjoy his other books, which are all available from Amazon.

Printed in Great Britain
by Amazon